Fun Word-Building Practice for Beginning Readers

- Word lists
- Craft ideas
- Individual activities
- Group activities
- Cards
- Patterns
- Skill sheets

Managing Editor: Lynn Drolet

Editorial Team: Becky S. Andrews, Diane Badden, Catherine Broome-Kehm, Kimberley Bruck, Karen A. Brudnak, Pam Crane, Pierce Foster, Tazmen Hansen, Marsha Heim, Lori Z. Henry, Lucia Kemp Henry, Debra Liverman, Kitty Lowrance, Jennifer Nunn, Gerri Primak, Mark Rainey, Greg D. Rieves, Kelly Robertson, Hope Rodgers, Eliseo De Jesus Santos II, Donna K. Teal, Rachael Traylor, Sharon M. Tresino

www.themailbox.com

ISBN10 #1-56234-930-9 • ISBN13 #978-1-56234-930-1

Printed in the United States
10 9 8 7 6 5 4 3 2 1

HPS 211912

TABLE OF CONTENTS

Single Word Families

Multiple Word Families

WHAT'S INSIDE

Practice with single word families

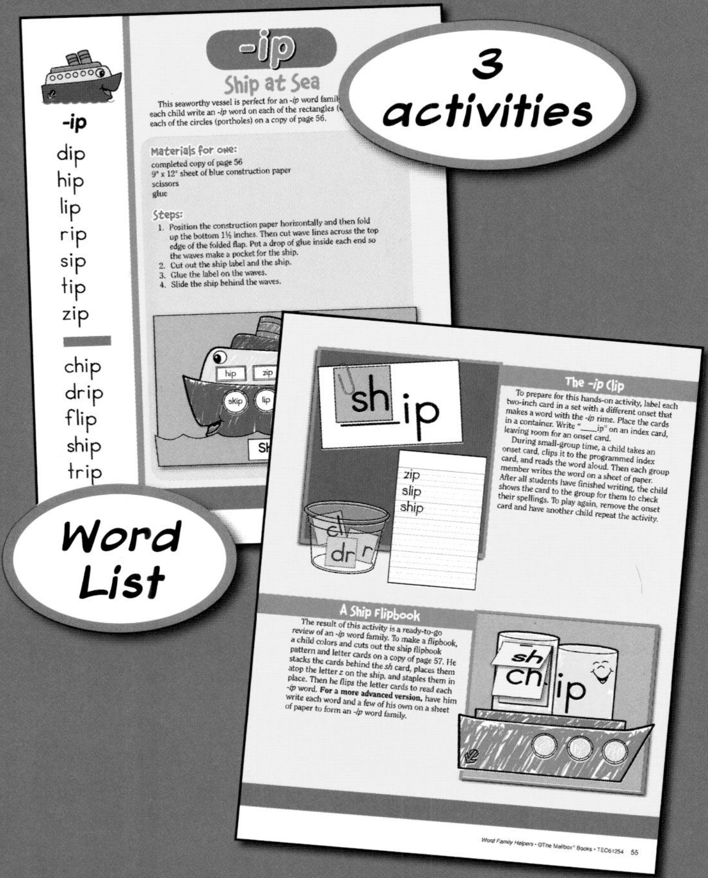

3 activities

Word List

3 reproducibles

Practice with multiple word families

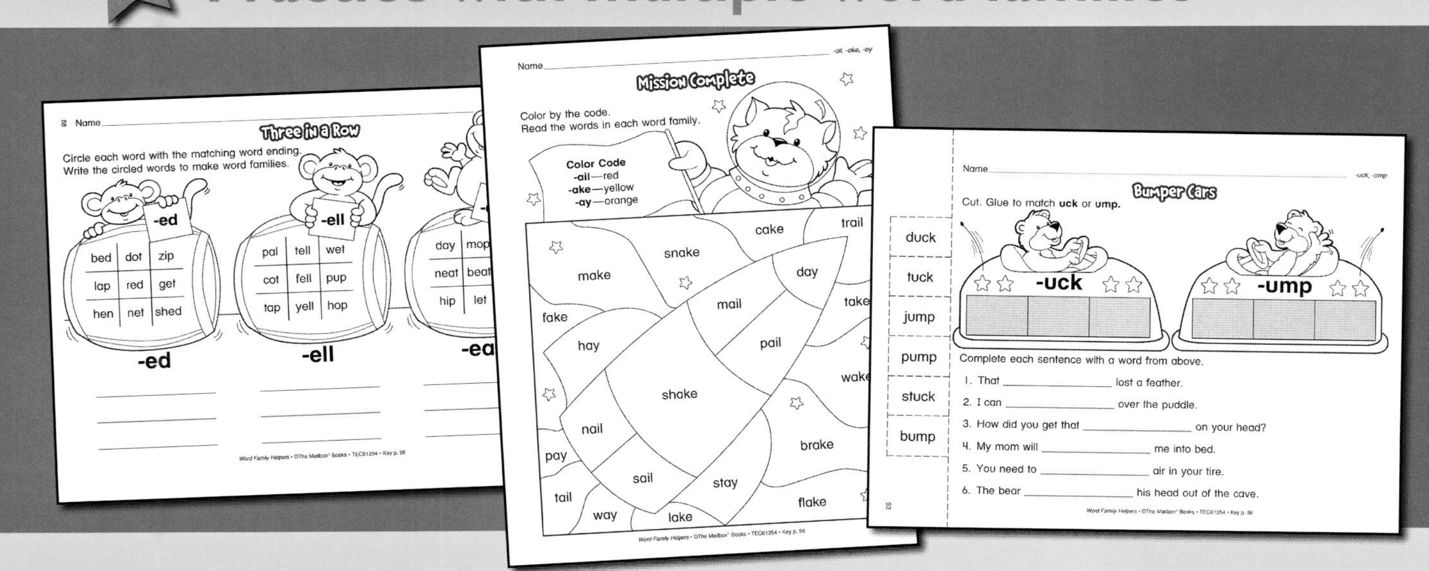

Name

Three in a Row

Circle each word with the matching word ending.
Write the circled words to make word families.

bed	dot	zip
lap	red	get
hen	net	shed

pal	tell	wet
cot	fell	pup
tap	yell	hop

-ed

-ell

Word Family Helpers • ©The Mailbox® Books • TEC61254 • Key p. 96

Name -ail, -ake, -ay

Mission Complete

Color by the code.
Read the words in each word family.

Color Code
-ail—red
-ake—yellow
-ay—orange

cake, trail, snake, make, day, mail, fake, take, hay, pail, shake, nail, pay, brake, sail, stay, tail, way, lake, flake

Word Family Helpers • ©The Mailbox® Books • TEC61254 • Key p. 96

Name -uck, -ump

Bumper Cars

Cut. Glue to match **uck** or **ump**.

duck, tuck, jump, pump, stuck, bump

-uck

-ump

Complete each sentence with a word from above.

1. That ______________ lost a feather.
2. I can ______________ over the puddle.
3. How did you get that ______________ on your head?
4. My mom will ______________ me into bed.
5. You need to ______________ air in your tire.
6. The bear ______________ his head out of the cave.

Word Family Helpers • ©The Mailbox® Books • TEC61254 • Key p. 96

-ack

back
pack
rack
sack
tack

black
crack
quack
shack
snack
stack
track

-ack

Pack Your Backpack

This backpack is a home for books that feature the *-ack* word family. To begin, have each child name the pictures on a copy of page 6 and write the corresponding words.

Materials for one:

completed copy of page 6
6″ x 18″ sheet of construction paper
two 1″ x 6″ strips of paper
scissors
glue

Steps:

1. Fold up the bottom of the construction paper sheet (set vertically) so it is three inches from the top. Then fold down the top three inches of the paper to make a flap.
2. Cut out the backpack label and glue it on the flap.
3. Round the bottom corners of the flap and the backpack.
4. Cut out the programmed books and glue them inside the backpack.
5. To add straps, refold the backpack and glue the ends of each paper strip to the back.

Let's Pack!

This small-group activity can be reused later for independent practice! Label individual cards with different words that end with *-ack*. Place the cards and a few unrelated word cards in the upper rows of a pocket chart. Set a backpack close by. Then invite each child, in turn, to read a word. If the word ends with *-ack,* she puts the card in the backpack; if not, she moves it to the bottom row. After the cards are sorted, remove the ones from the backpack and lead the group in rereading each word. Encourage each youngster to write his own list of *-ack* words at a center.

Super Sack

Program a folded paper lunch sack with an onset box and the rime *-ack* as shown. Write on index cards onsets that form real and nonsense words when paired with the rime. Set the sack, cards, and a paper rectangle for each child at a center.

To begin, a child trims the top of a paper rectangle so it resembles a sack and writes "-ack" at the top. Then he places an onset card in the box on the lunch sack. If a real word is formed, he writes the word on his paper. If not, he sets the card aside. He continues with each remaining onset card to form an *-ack* word family. **For an easier version,** do not include onset cards that form nonsense words.

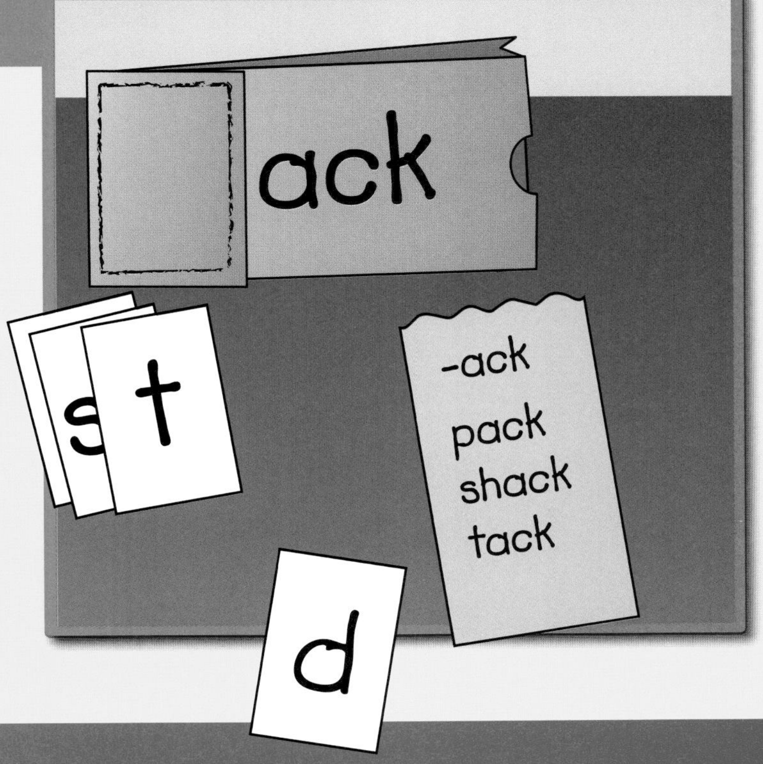

Backpack Label and Book Patterns

Use with "Pack Your Backpack" on page 4.

Pack Your Backpack

TEC61254

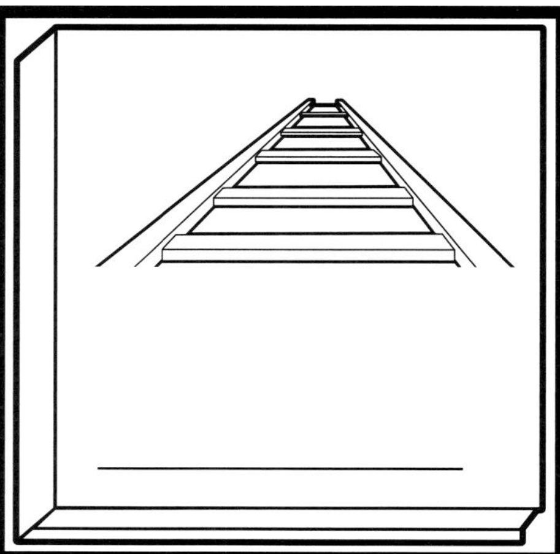

JUICE

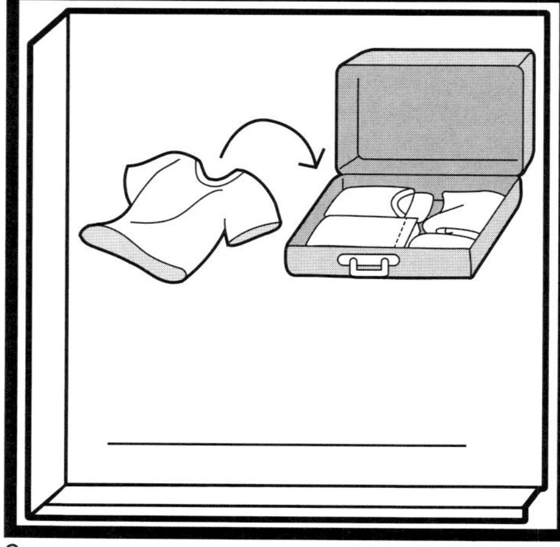

Name______________________________

Back on Track

Cut.
Glue to match.

Name ____________________

A Fine Snack

Name each picture.
Color the **ack** words.
Write the **ack** words.

-ack

____________________ ____________________

____________________ ____________________

____________________ ____________________

____________________ ____________________

Mail for Snail

This envelope stores words from the *-ail* word family. To prepare, have each child write a different *-ail* word on each snail card from a copy of page 11.

Materials for one:

completed copy of page 11
envelope
scissors
glue

Steps:

1. Cut out the label, stamp, and snail cards.
2. Glue the label and stamp on the envelope.
3. Read the word on each snail card and place it in the envelope.

-ail

fail
jail
mail
nail
pail
rail
sail
tail

frail
quail
snail
trail

Sign That Pail!

Here's a group activity that results in a take-home review. To prepare, write "__ail" on the board as shown. Then draw a simple pail shape around the text. Have each student write *"-ail"* at the top of a paper pail shape. If desired, have her attach a pipe cleaner to make a handle. To begin, write an onset on the blank line. Invite a child to blend the word parts to determine whether it is a real word or a nonsense word. If it is a real word, she says, "Sign that pail!" and each youngster copies the word onto her pail. Continue in this manner until several real words are formed. Then encourage youngsters to take their pails home to reread the *-ail* word family.

Stand-Up Snail

Students reveal different *-ail* words with this craft. Precut the slits on a class supply of copies of page 12. A student colors and cuts out his snail and letter strip. He cuts antennae from the paper scraps and then glues them to the snail. Next, he folds the bottom of the snail back along the fold line and then threads the strip though the slits, keeping the letters forward. He glues the ends of the strip where indicated to make a stand for the snail. To form a new *-ail* word, he slides the stand to change the onset and writes each word on a sheet of paper.

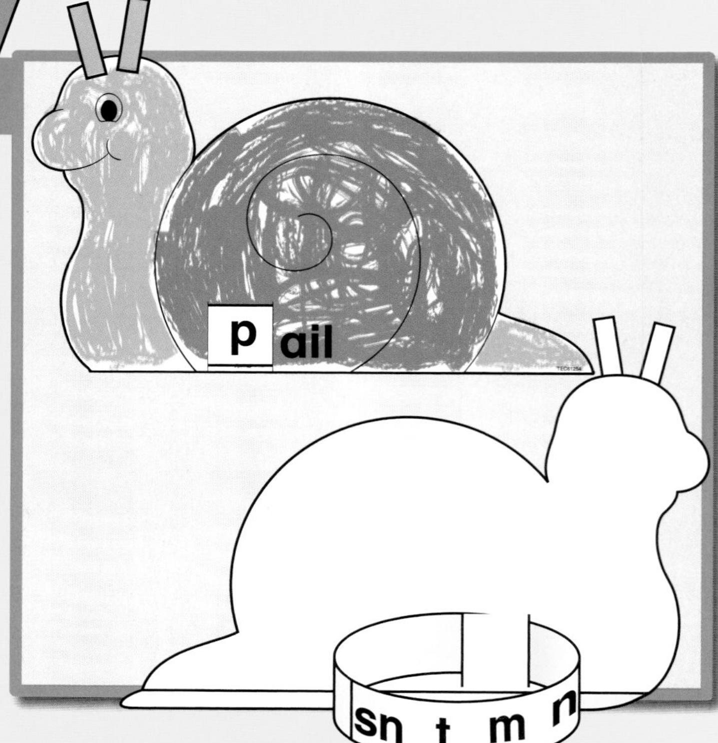

Use with "Mail for Snail" on page 9.

Snail Pattern and Letter Strip

Use with "Stand-Up Snail" on page 10.

Ready, Set, Sail

Write **ail** on each line.
Cut.
Glue to match.

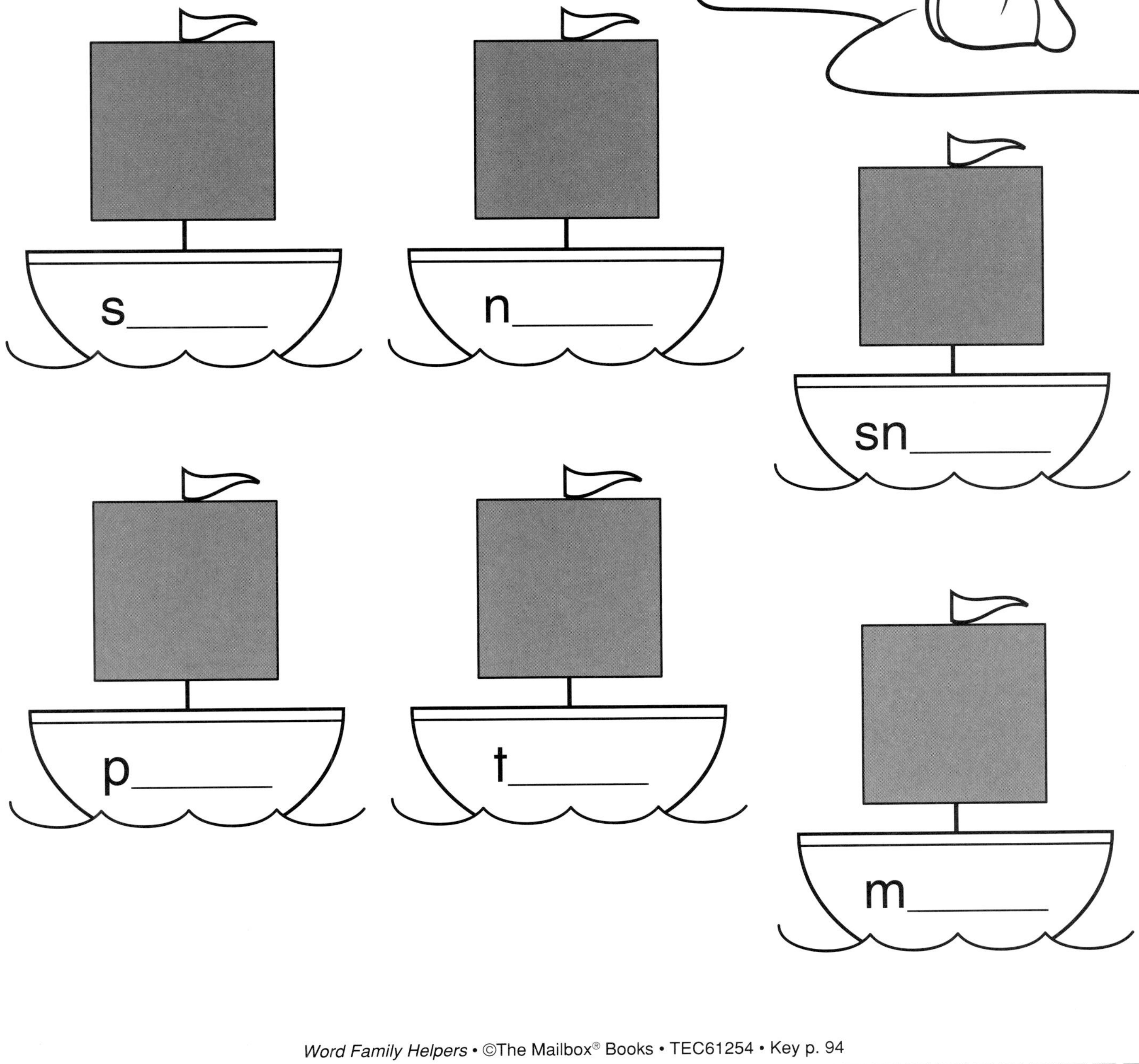

s______

n______

sn______

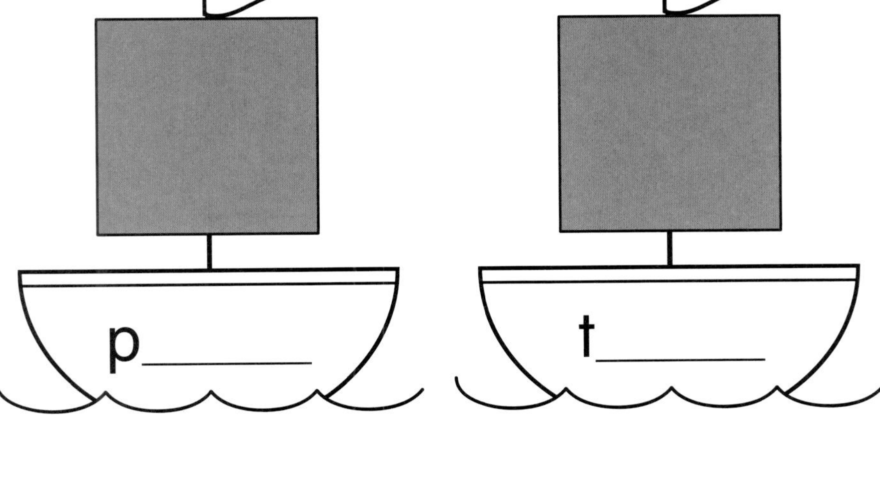

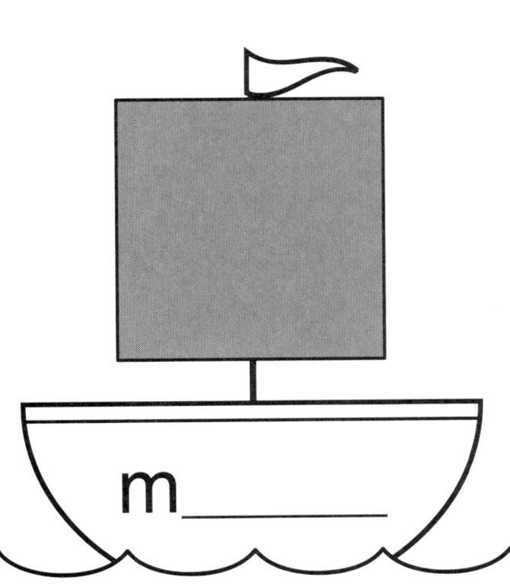

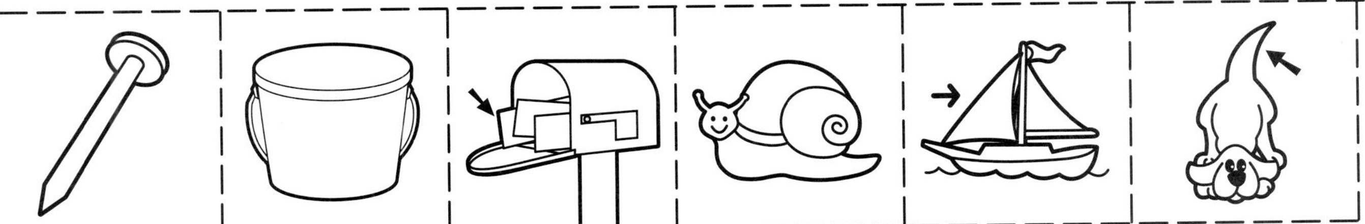

-ake

bake
cake
fake
lake
make
rake
take
wake

brake
flake
shake
snake

Snake's Cake

The random order of these *-ake* words makes each snake one of a kind! Give each child a copy of page 16. Have each child write *-ake* words on the three snake patterns. Then have him lightly color the snake.

Materials for one:

completed copy of page 16
6" x 6" paper square
scissors
crayons
glue

Steps:

1. Cut out the snake patterns and label.
2. Make a line of glue along the top, middle, and bottom of the square (cake). Glue the snake cutouts to the cake so the snake appears to be coiled around the cake.
3. Glue the label on the cake.
4. Draw cake details.

Layer Cake

To prepare for this small-group activity, draw a layered cake on a sheet of chart paper and label the top section as shown. Write on candle cutouts (pattern on page 17) different onsets that form -*ake* words. To form an -*ake* word family, have each child, in turn, put a candle to the left of the rime, read the word, and write it on a layer of the cake. Then have the group read the completed cake. **For an added challenge,** include distracter onsets that form nonsense words.

Make a Snake

Reinforce -*ake* words with this puzzle. Have each child read the words on the snake puzzle pieces on a copy of page 17. Instruct her to lightly color each puzzle piece that has an -*ake* word. Then have her color the head, carefully cut out the colored pieces, and discard the unrelated words. After she assembles the pieces to make a snake, direct her to glue the snake to a 4" x 12" sheet of paper. **For a home-school connection,** encourage her to take the snake home to read the -*ake* words to a family member.

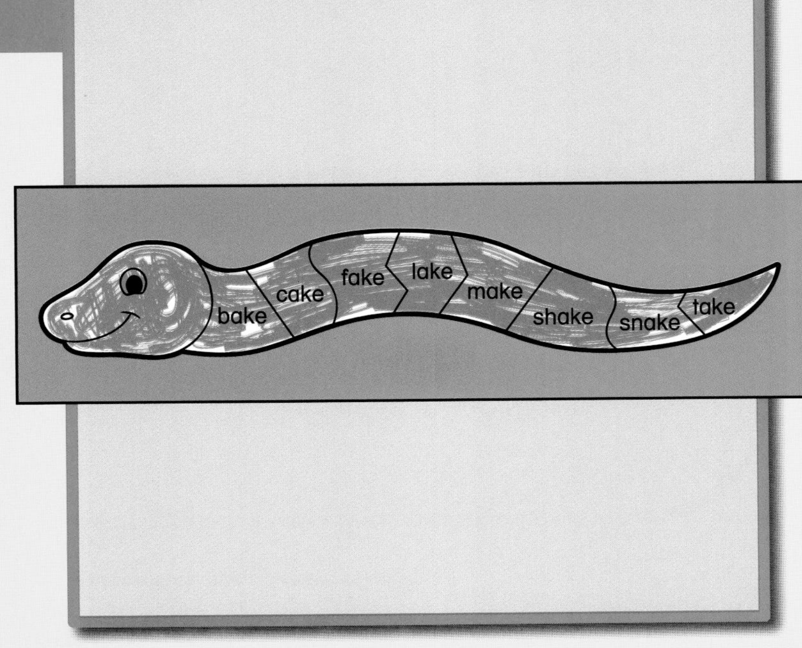

Snake Patterns and Label

Use with "Snake's Cake" on page 14.

Snake's Cake

TEC61254

Candle Pattern

Use with "Layer Cake" on page 15.

TEC61254

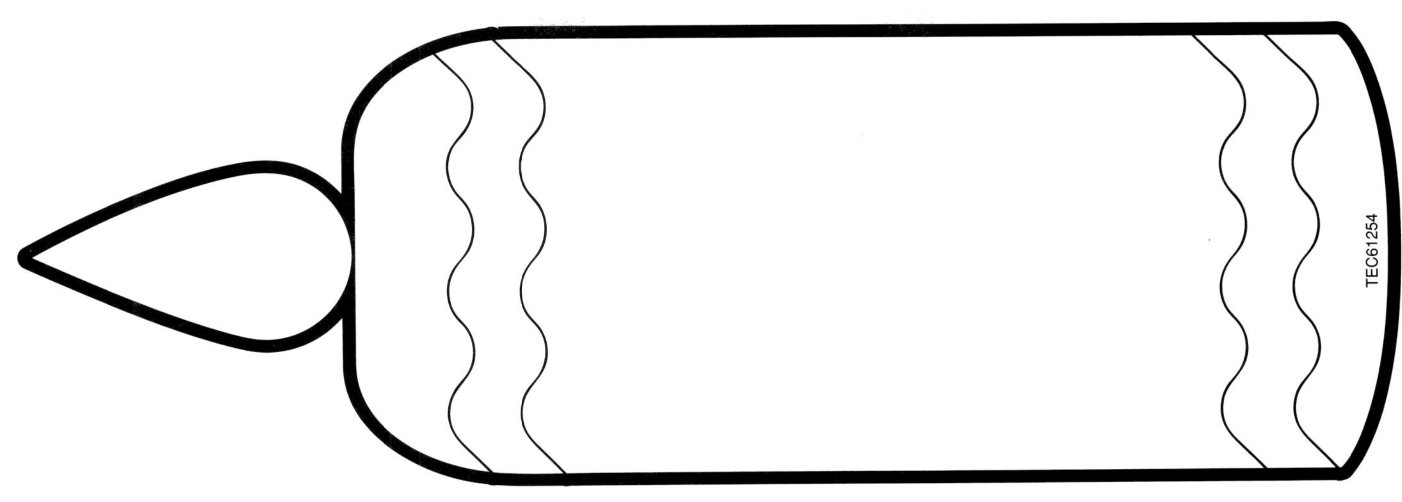

Snake Puzzle Pieces

Use with "Make a Snake" on page 15.

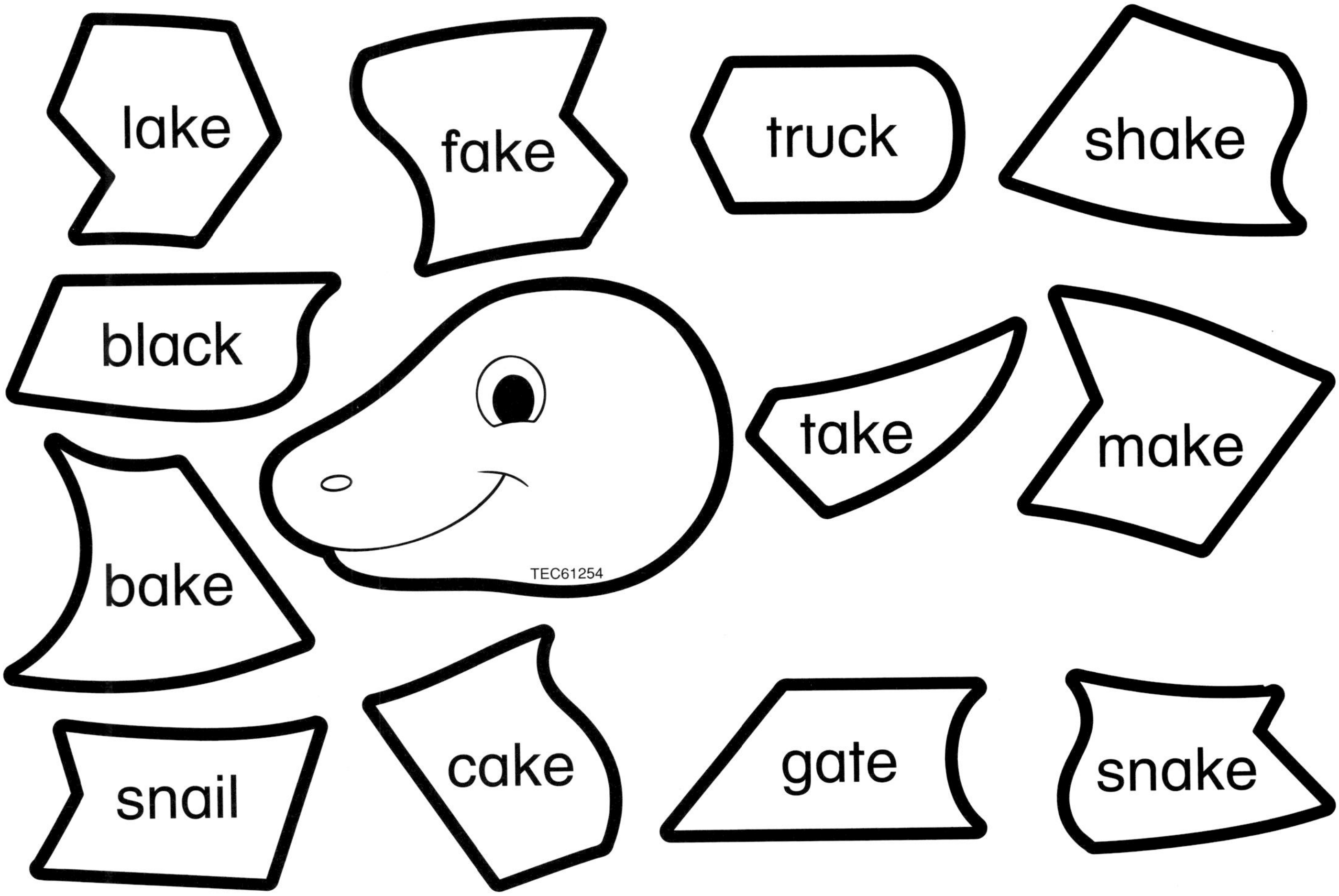

lake
fake
truck
shake
black
take
make
bake
TEC61254
cake
gate
snail
snake

Name ______________________________ *-ake*

Shake for Snake

Write **ake** on each line.
Circle the real words.

b________

m________

h________

sn________

z________

w________

r________

pl________

Complete each sentence with a circled word from above.

1. There is a green ______________ in the garden.
2. I like to ______________ cookies in the oven.
3. My dad will ______________ the leaves.
4. Did you ______________ this mess?
5. What time did you ______________ this morning?

Painter's Cap

The paint spots on this cap are a perfect canvas for an *-ap* word family! To prepare, have each child write a different *-ap* word on each of eight colorful two-inch paper squares.

Materials for one:

student-programmed paper squares
cap pattern (page 21)
scissors
glue

Steps:

1. Cut out the cap.
2. Trim each paper square, carefully cutting away from the word, so the paper resembles a spot of paint.
3. Arrange the paint spots on the cap so the words are horizontal and glue them in place.

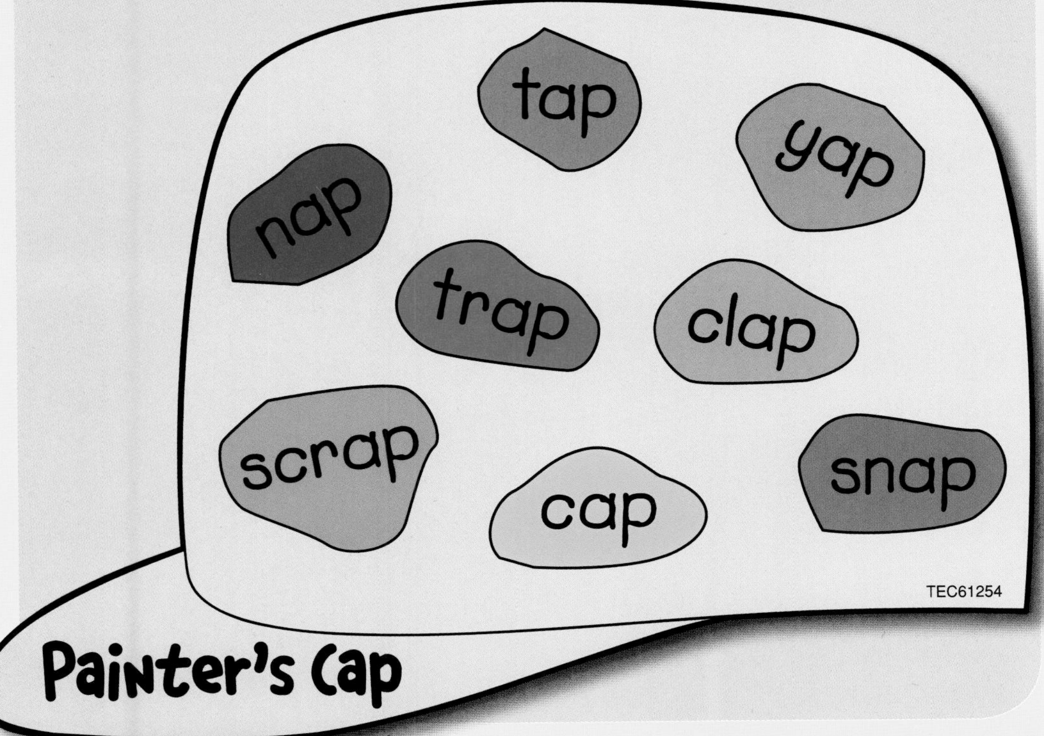

-ap

cap
lap
map
nap
tap
yap

clap
flap
snap
trap

scrap
strap

Clap for -ap!

The lively response in this phonological activity engages every learner. To begin, invite two or three students, in turn, to name *-ap* words. For each correct word, respond by clapping. Then change roles! Name different words, most of which end with the rime *-ap*. For each *-ap* word, have your youngsters clap. For practice on another day, change the response to snapping fingers or flapping arms. Students are sure to recognize *-ap* words with a clap, snap, or flap!

Yap! Yap!

Students find out what the puppy has to say with this center activity. Color and cut out a copy of the puppy pattern and onset wheel on page 22. Use a brad to attach the wheel behind the puppy where indicated, making sure *-ap* words are formed when the wheel is turned. If desired, have each child assemble her own word wheel.

At the center, a child writes *"-ap"* at the top of a paper strip. Then she spins the wheel to make a word, reads it, and writes it on her paper. She continues in this manner to form an *-ap* word family.

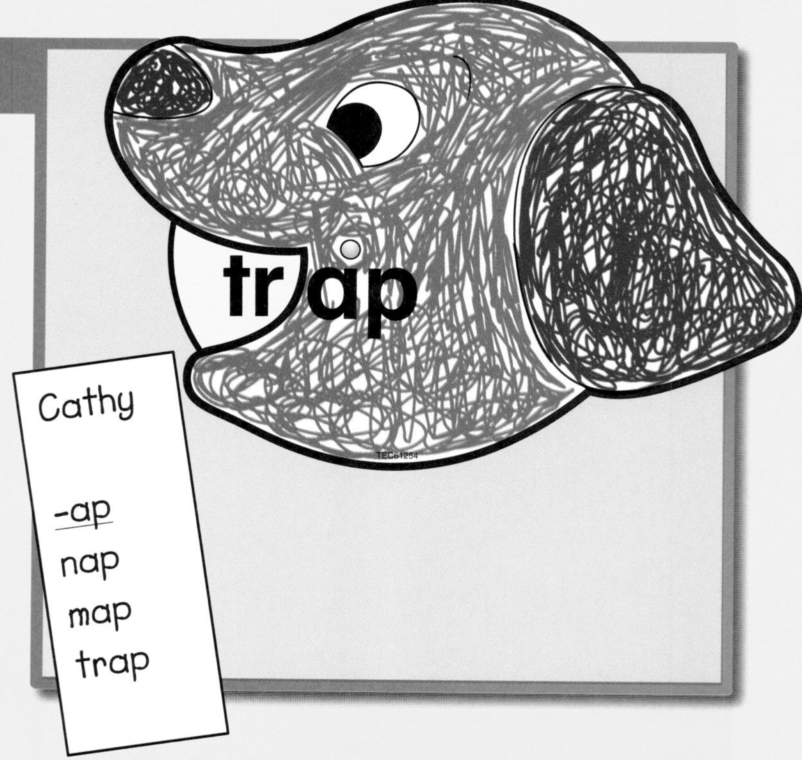

Cap Pattern

Use with "Painter's Cap" on page 19.

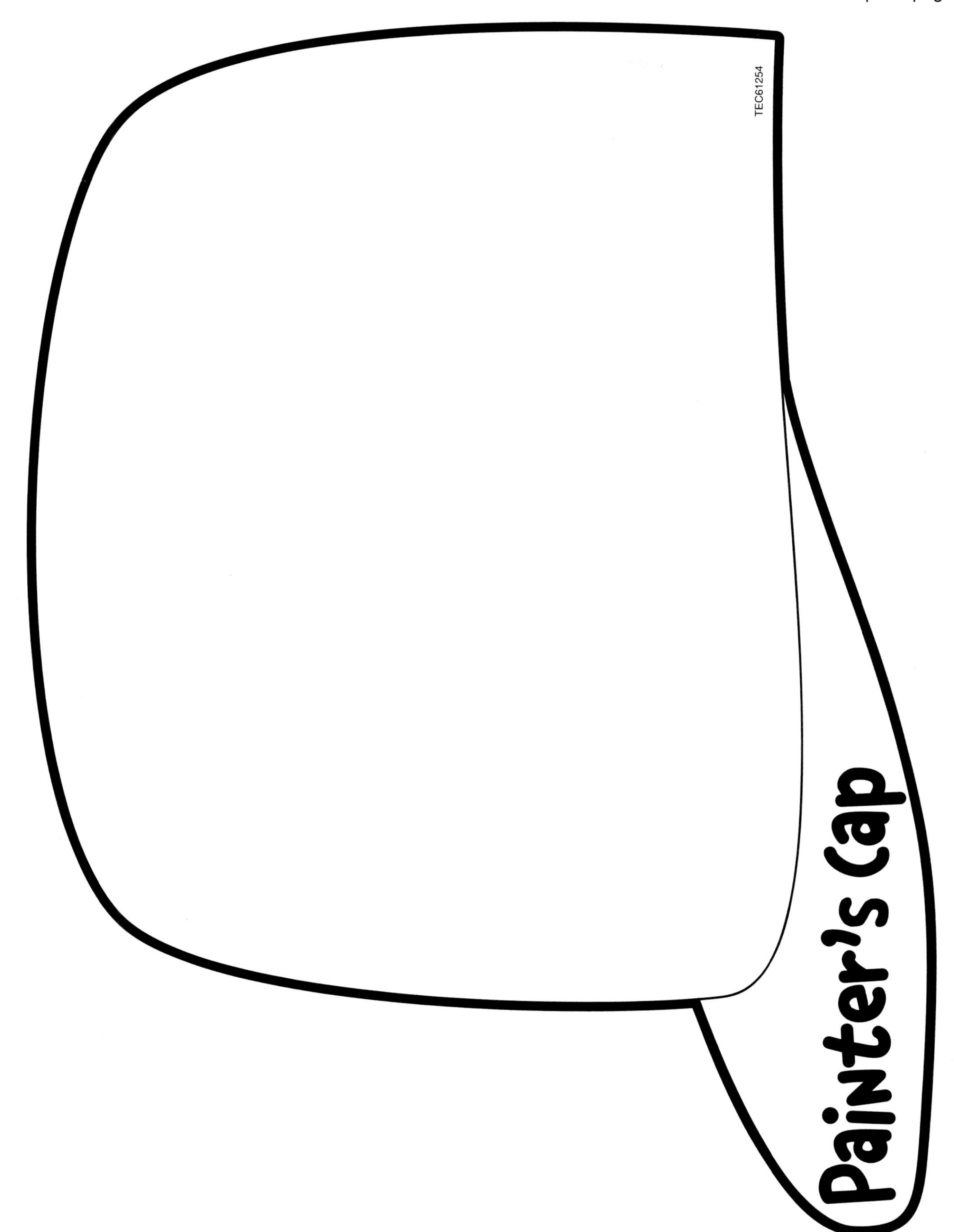

Puppy Pattern and Onset Wheel

Use with "Yap! Yap!" on page 20.

Name ____________________ *-ap*

Afternoon Nap

Write **ap** on each line.
Circle the real words.

-ay
day
hay
lay
may
pay
ray
say

clay
play
stay
tray

spray

Hooray for Hay!

This horse stall stores hay bales that provide a handy review of *-ay* words. To begin, give each child yellow copies of pages 26 and 27. Then have each youngster write a different *-ay* word on each hay bale.

Materials for one:

completed copies of pages 26 and 27
5" x 12" brown construction paper
stapler
scissors
glue

Steps:

1. Cut out the horse card, label, and hay bale cards.
2. Glue the horse card near the top of the vertically aligned construction paper.
3. Fold up the bottom 2½ inches of the paper and staple the sides.
4. Glue the label on the resulting pocket and place the hay bales inside.
5. Add details to the project so it looks like a horse stall.

play
may
Hooray for Hay!

Pass the Tray

To prepare for this group activity, write a different *-ay* word on each of several cards and then place them facedown on a tray. Gather students in a circle. Lead youngsters in the chant shown as they pass the tray around the circle. At the end of the chant, the child holding the tray chooses a card, reads the word, and says, "I can say [word on card]." Then he returns the card facedown to the tray. Continue as time allows.

Can you say? Can you say
One little word that ends with *-ay?*

Rays of Sunshine

Invite students to make sunny reminders of *-ay* words. Have each youngster sponge-paint a paper plate so it looks like a sun. When the paint is dry, direct her to write *-ay* in the center of her plate. Then have her write a different *-ay* word on each of several yellow paper strips (rays) and glue each ray to her plate to complete her sun.

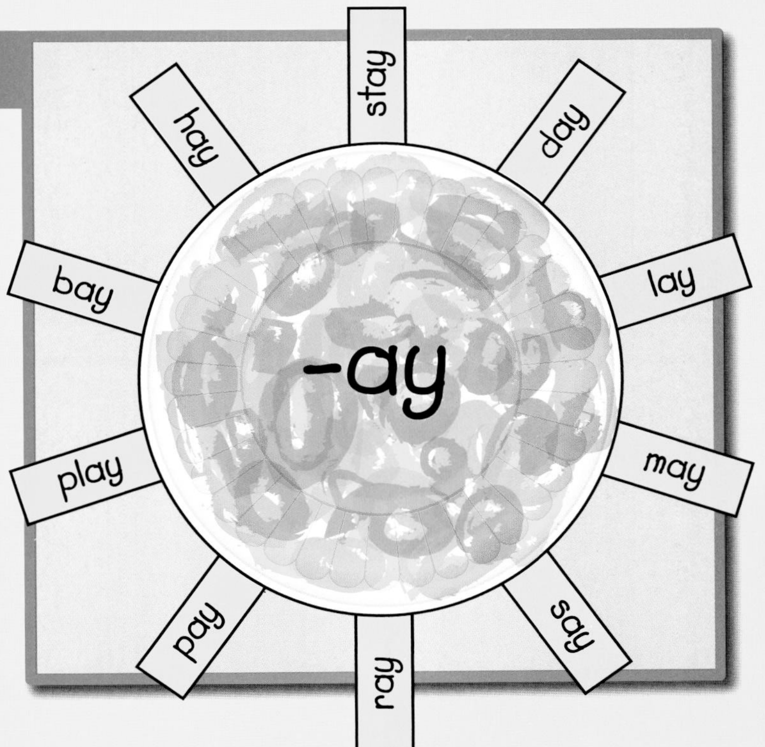

Horse Card, Label, and Hay Bale Cards

Use with "Hooray for Hay!" on page 24.

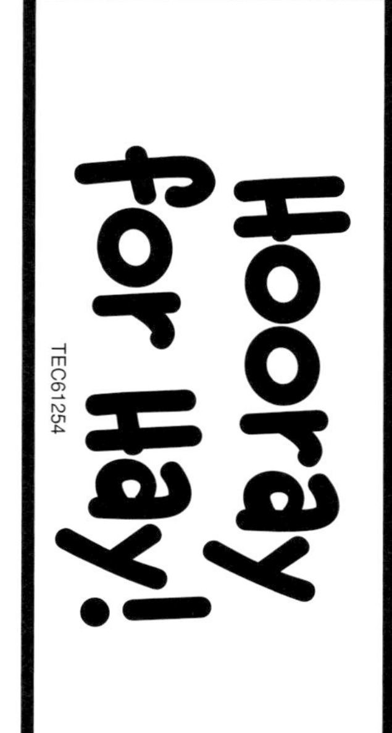

TEC61254

TEC61254

TEC61254

TEC61254

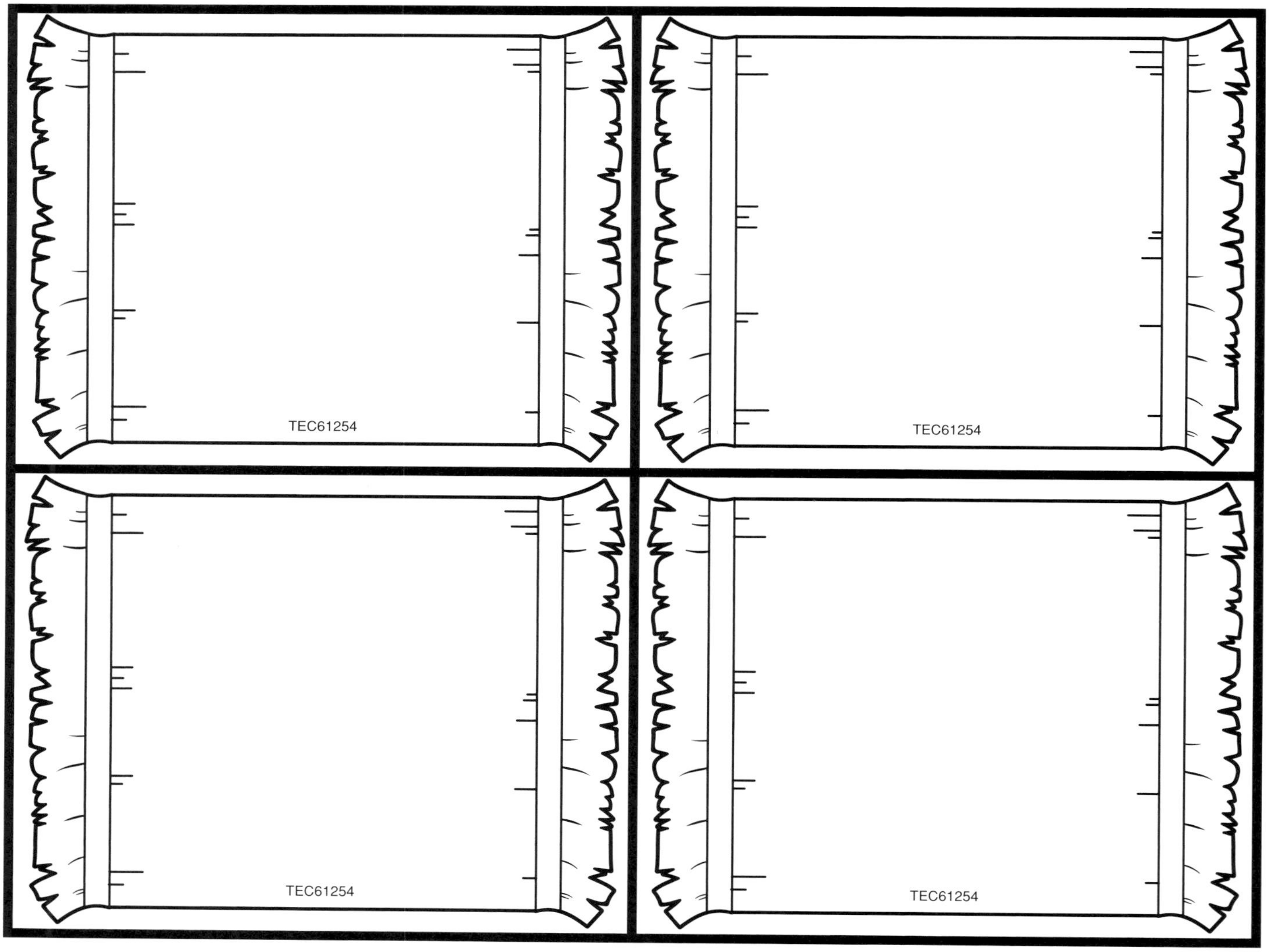

Hay Bale Cards

Use with "Hooray for Hay!" on page 24.

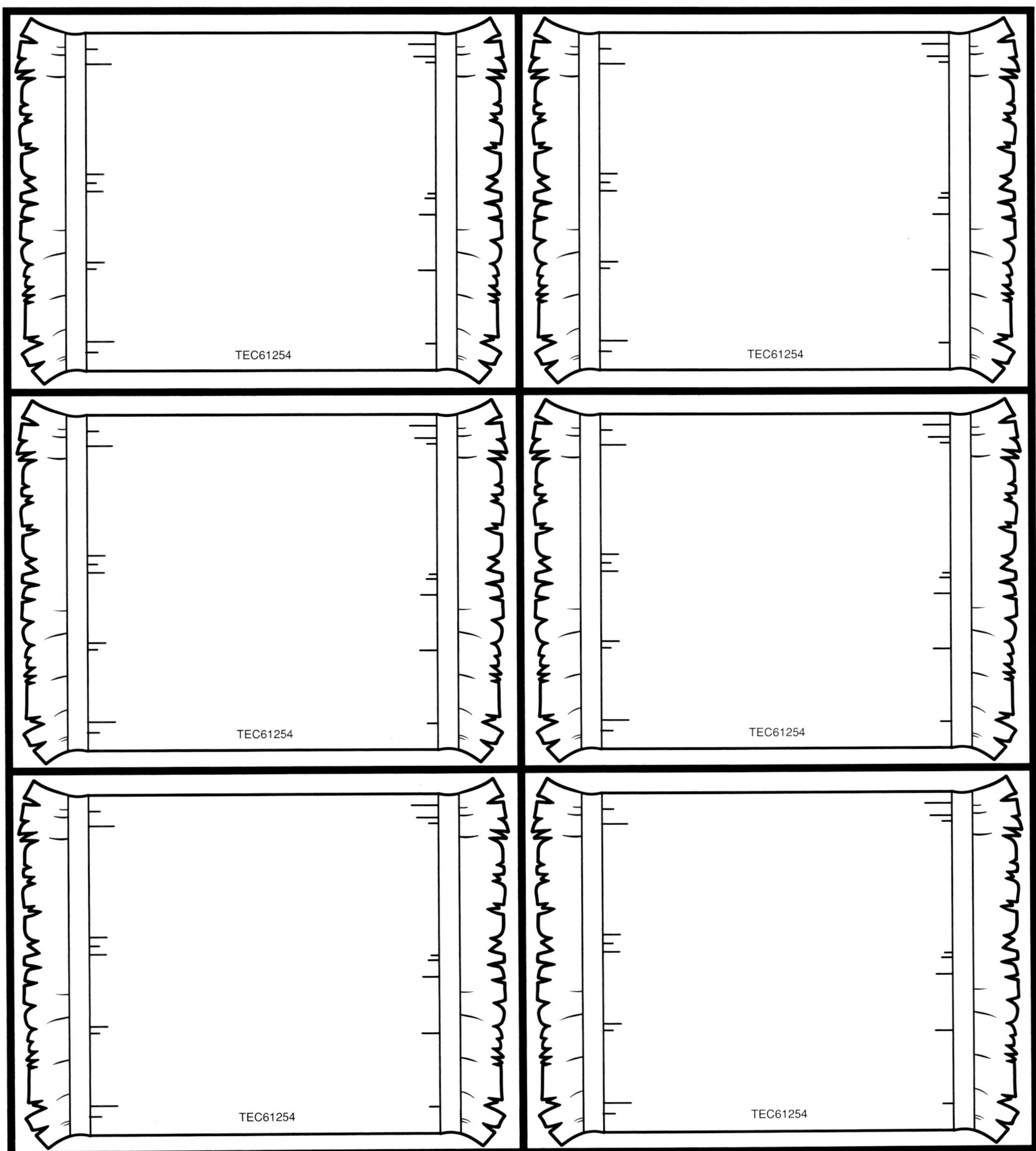

Name ______________________________ -ay

What a Spray!

Color each real **ay** word.

Write each real **ay** word from above.

1. ______________ 2. ______________

3. ______________ 4. ______________

5. ______________ 6. ______________

7. ______________ 8. ______________

My Treat Jar

When a child takes the treats from this jar, he practices reading *-eat* words! To begin, have each child trace the *-eat* words on a copy of page 31.

Materials for one:

completed copy of page 31
4½" x 12" construction paper strip
glue
scissors

Steps:

1. Fold the construction paper strip vertically until the bottom edge is about one inch from the top. Fold the top portion down over the edge.
2. Trim the corners to make a jar shape.
3. Open the top flap and then glue the side edges of the paper together to make a pocket.
4. Fold the top flap down and draw lines on it so it resembles a lid.
5. Cut out the label and treat cards. Glue the label to the jar. Store the treat cards in the jar.

-eat

beat
heat
meat
neat
seat

---

bleat
cheat
cleat
pleat
treat
wheat

Have a Seat!

Students take a seat to respond to *-eat* words during this group game. Prepare a set of word cards in which some words are in the *-eat* word family and some are not. To begin, have each child stand by a chair. Then show and read a word card. If the word ends with the rime *-eat,* students quickly take a seat; if it does not, students remain standing. Continue with different words, making sure students are standing before reading each word. **For a more advanced version,** silently show a word card for students to respond to and then invite a child to read the word aloud.

Monster Munch

The hungry critter at this center likes to eat *-eat* words! To prepare, label a supply of cards with words, most of which end with the rime *-eat.* Then decorate a shoebox with craft supplies to make a monster similar to the one shown. (Be sure to cut a mouth slot that is larger than your word cards.)

When a child visits the center, she reads a word card and identifies the rime. If the word ends with *-eat,* she feeds it to the monster. If it does not, she sets the card aside. She continues with each remaining card. Then she reviews the monster's treats and writes each word on a sheet of paper to form an *-eat* word family.

Label and Treat Cards

Use with "My Treat Jar" on page 29.

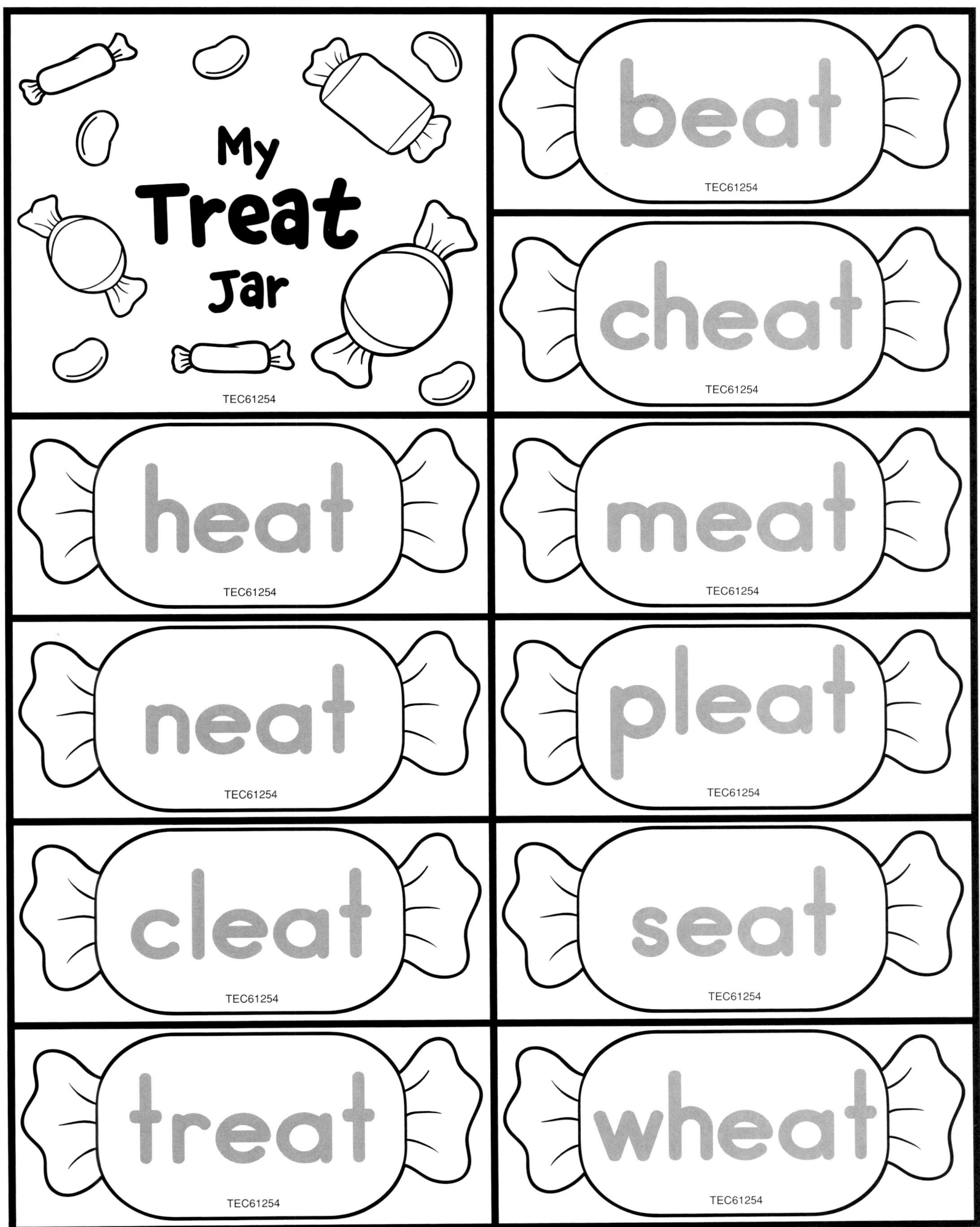

Name ______________________

Eat That Treat!

Write **eat** to complete each word.
Color the real words.
Write the real words on the lines below.

1. ______________________ 5. ______________________

2. ______________________ 6. ______________________

3. ______________________ 7. ______________________

4. ______________________ 8. ______________________

Name ________________________________ *-eat*

Feel the Heat!

Color the **eat** words.

Complete each sentence with a colored word from above.

1. The turtle ________________ the rabbit in the race.
2. Do not ________________ on the test.
3. I like to keep my desk clean and ________________.
4. My dad put the dish in the oven to ________________ our dinner.
5. When we stopped at the pet store, my dog got a ________________.

-est

best
jest
nest
pest
rest
test
vest
west
zest

chest
guest
quest

Treasure Chest

The gems in this chest form an *-est* word family! To prepare, have each child write "est" to complete each word on a copy of page 36.

Materials for one:

completed copy of page 36
9" x 12" sheet of construction paper
paper scraps
scissors
glue

Steps:

1. Position the paper vertically and fold up the bottom so it ends four inches from the top. Glue both the left and right edges of the folded flap to make a pocket (chest).
2. Fold down the top of the paper to meet the folded edge (lid). Cut the top two corners to round them.
3. Cut out the treasure chest label and glue it on the lid. Use paper scraps to add treasure chest details.
4. Cut out the gem cards and read each one aloud before storing it in the chest.

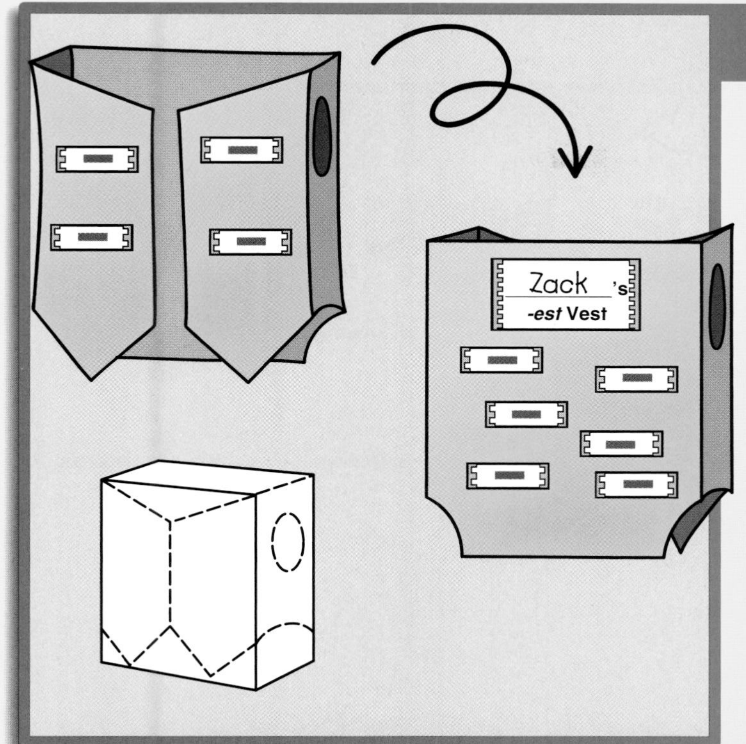

The -est Vest

Students can wear this *-est* word family home! To make a paper vest, help each child cut a grocery bag up the middle of a large panel, cut away the bottom, and then trim the bag to resemble a vest as shown. Next, help him cut on each of the smaller panels a hole large enough for his arm. Then instruct him to cut out the vest label and word cards on a copy of page 37 and glue them to his vest. Encourage him to wear the vest to display his *-est* word family.

Nifty Nest

The nest egg at this center helps students write *-est* words. Write "-est" on a class supply of egg cutouts. Place the prepared eggs at a center along with blank paper, brown paper strips, and glue. When a child visits the center, she glues strips near the top of her paper to make a nest. Next, she glues an egg to the nest. Then, she writes *-est* words on her paper to form a word family.

Treasure Chest Label and Gem Cards

Use with "Treasure Chest" on page 34.

Treasure Chest
TEC61254

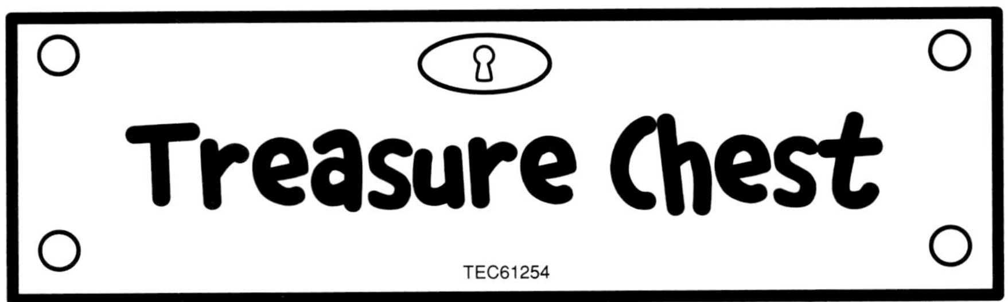

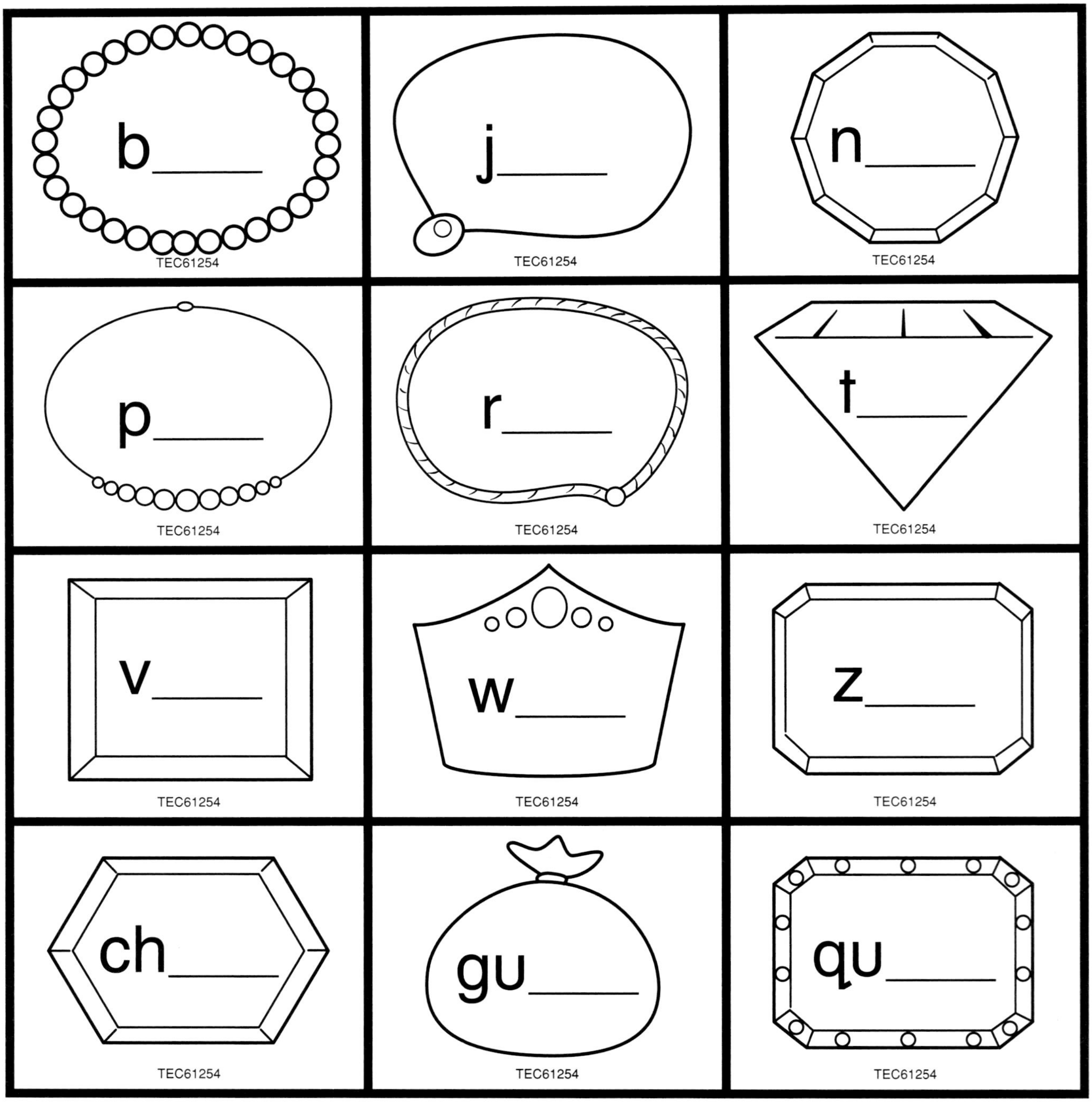

b____
TEC61254
j____
TEC61254
n____
TEC61254
p____
TEC61254
r____
TEC61254
t____
TEC61254
v____
TEC61254
w____
TEC61254
z____
TEC61254
ch____
TEC61254
gu____
TEC61254
qu____
TEC61254

Vest Label and Word Cards

Use with "The *-est* Vest" on page 35.

best	nest
pest	rest
test	vest
west	zest
chest	guest

Clown's Best Vest

Complete each word below. Use the letters to help you.
Write the word that answers each riddle.

v b ch r n w

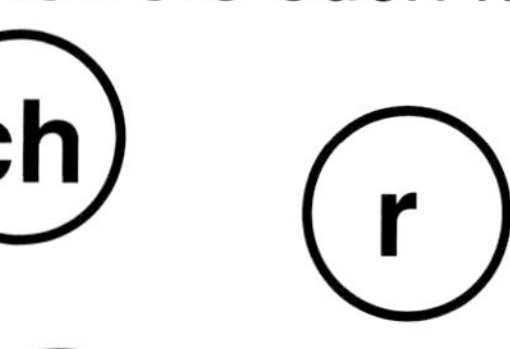

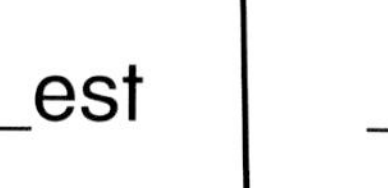

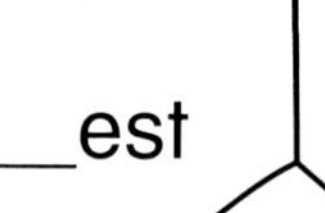

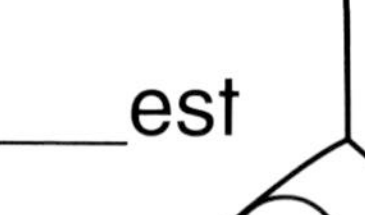
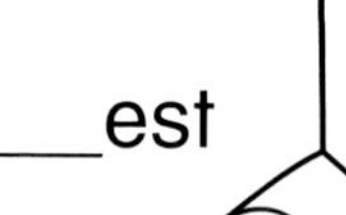

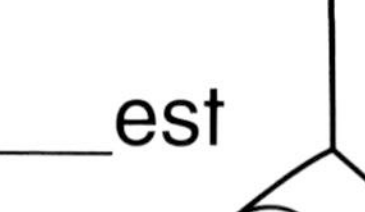

____est ____est

____est ____est

____est ____est

1. A bird likes to sit on me.

   ____

2. I am a part of your body.

   ____

3. You can wear me.

   ____

4. You do this when you are tired.

   ____

5. I am not east, north, or south. I am

   ____________________.

6. When you try really hard, you try your

   ____________________.

-ick

A Hideout for Chick

This chicken coop not only conceals an adorable chick but also gives a quick review of *-ick* words. To begin, give each child a copy of page 41. Have her write a different *-ick* word in each box.

Materials for one:

completed copy of page 41
4½" x 12" brown construction paper
brown construction paper scraps
scissors
glue

Steps:

1. Cut out the label, chick card, and word box pattern.
2. Fold the construction paper so the bottom edge is about one inch from the top.
3. Open the paper. Glue the chick card above the fold and the word list below the fold.
4. Glue the label above the chick card, leaving the bottom portion unattached.
5. To hide the chick, refold the paper, tucking the edge under the label.
6. Cut two small rectangles from the construction paper scraps and glue them to the bottom of the folded paper to finish the chicken coop.

-ick

kick
lick
pick
sick

brick
chick
click
flick
slick
stick
thick
trick

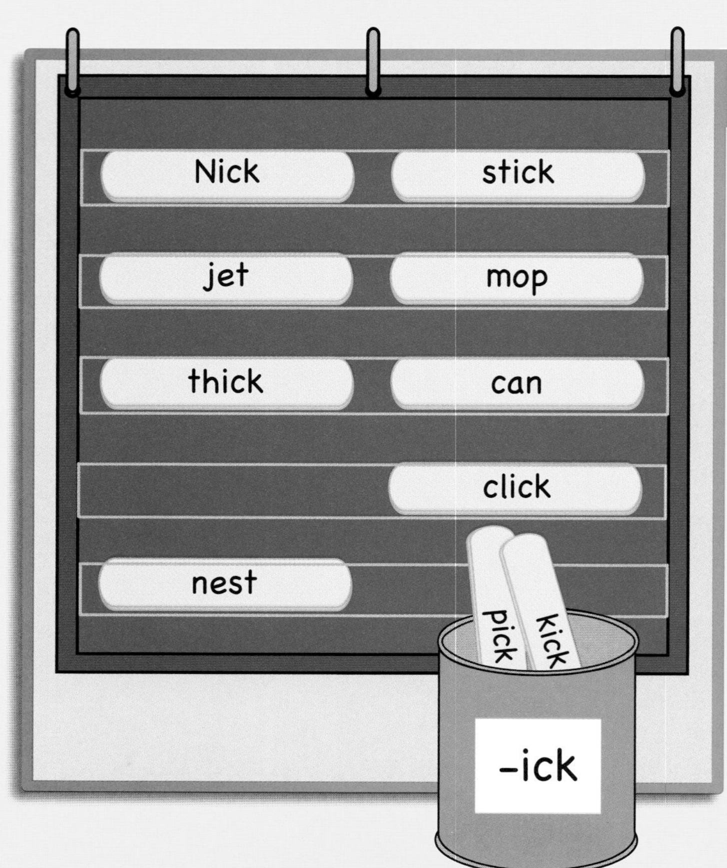

Pick a Stick

To prepare for this small-group activity, program a supply of jumbo craft sticks with some words that are in the *-ick* word family and some that are not. Place the sticks in a pocket chart and label a container as shown. Call a child to the pocket chart as you lead the group in chanting, "[Child's name, child's name], pick a stick that sounds like *-ick!*" Then have the child choose a stick labeled with an *-ick* word, read the word aloud, and place the stick in the container. Continue until all the sticks labeled with *-ick* words have been placed in the container.

Brick by Brick

At this center, youngsters build word family skills one brick at a time! In advance, program one small block (brick) with the rime *-ick* and at least eight additional blocks with a variety of onsets. A child visits the center and manipulates the bricks to form words. She writes each real *-ick* word she makes on a copy of a recording sheet from page 42.

Label, Chick Card, and Word Box Pattern

Use with "A Hideout for Chick" on page 39.

Name ______________________________ *-ick*

Brick by Brick

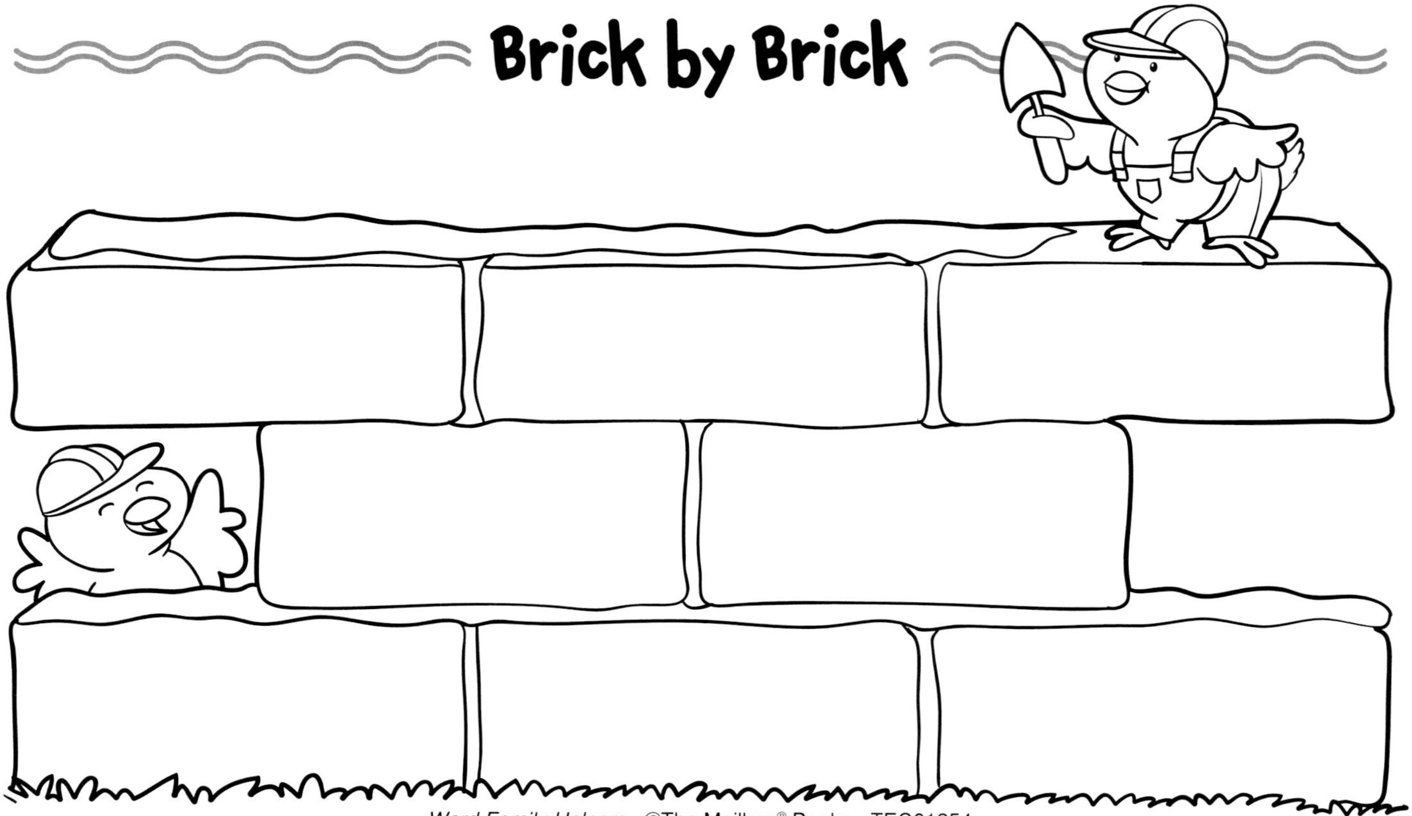

Word Family Helpers • ©The Mailbox® Books • TEC61254

Name ______________________________ *-ick*

Brick by Brick

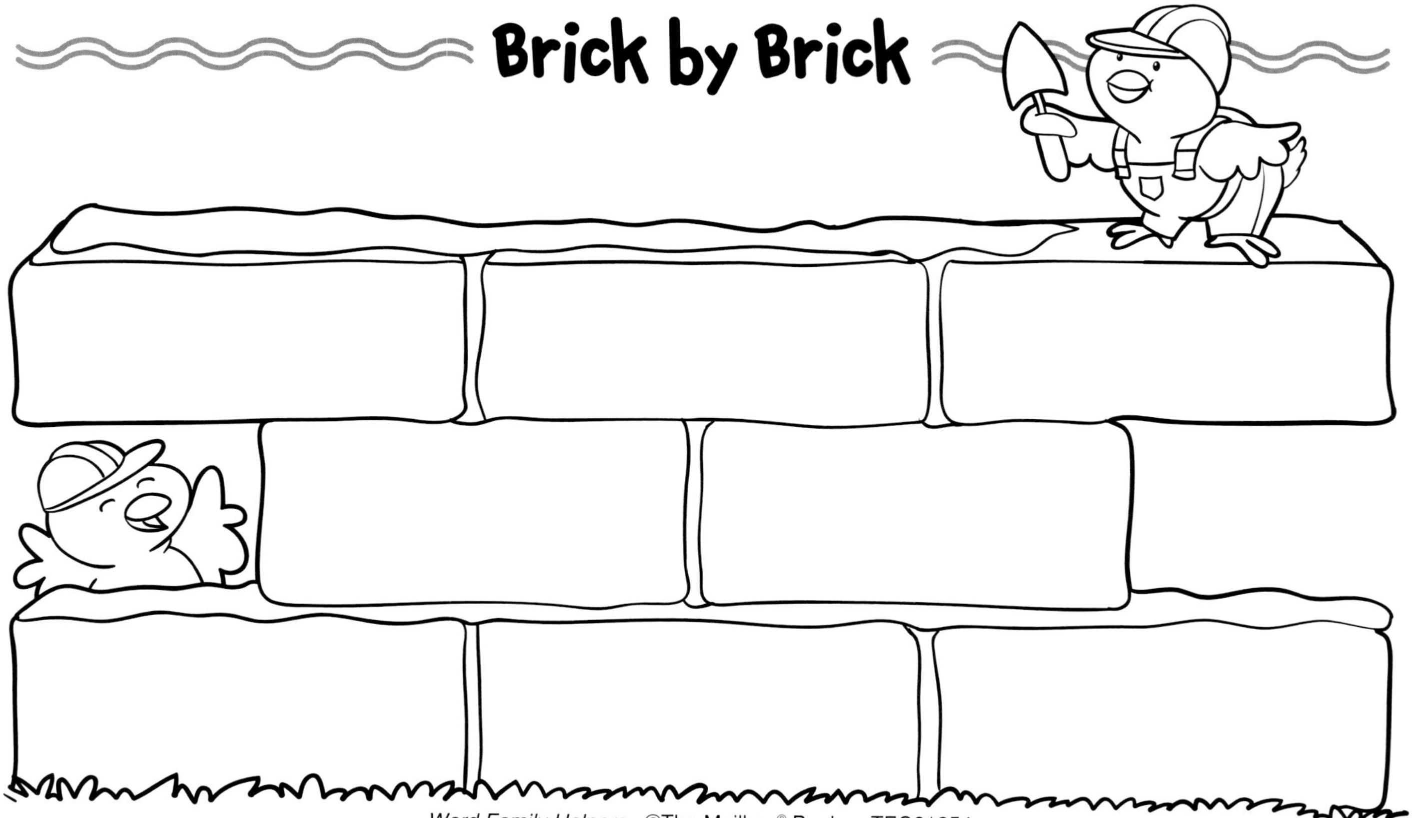

Word Family Helpers • ©The Mailbox® Books • TEC61254

 Note to the teacher: Use with "Brick by Brick" on page 40.

Name ____________________

What a Trick!

Write **ick** to finish each word.

ch__________ s__________ p__________

k__________ tr__________ br__________

Complete each sentence with a word from above.

1. Did you ______________ this pretty flower?
2. The fuzzy ______________ is cute.
3. I live in a ______________ house.
4. My friend is feeling ______________ today.
5. Sam is going to ______________ the ball.
6. I learned a new magic ______________.

-ight

fight
light
might
night
right
sight
tight

bright
flight
fright
knight
slight

A Mighty Knight

This brave knight gives students practice writing *-ight* words. To begin, have each child write eight to ten *-ight* words on a copy of the shield pattern from page 46.

Materials for one:

- completed copy of page 46
- sheet of construction paper
- masking tape
- scissors
- crayons
- glue

Steps:

1. Cut out the label, knight, and shield patterns.
2. Glue the label to the top of the paper and glue the knight to the bottom.
3. Make a loop with a piece of masking tape and place it on the knight's lower hand. Attach the shield to the knight.
4. Draw details to complete the knight.

A Bright Light

Students' word work shines at this center. Program a supply of cards with *-ight* words and some words that are not in the *-ight* word family. Place the cards at a center along with a class supply of large lightbulb cutouts. A child reads the word on a card. If it is an *-ight* word, he writes the word on his lightbulb cutout. If not, he sets the card aside. He continues with the remaining cards.

Read the Shield

This knight's shield is spun to reveal *-ight* words. From a class supply of page 47, precut the small square on the shield on each page. Then provide a page to each child and have her color and cut out the knight and letter wheel patterns. Have her place the letter wheel behind the shield so the dots align. Then help her insert a brad through both pieces where indicated. A child turns the wheel, reads each *-ight* word, and writes it on a sheet of paper.

Label and Knight and Shield Patterns

Use with "A Mighty Knight" on page 44.

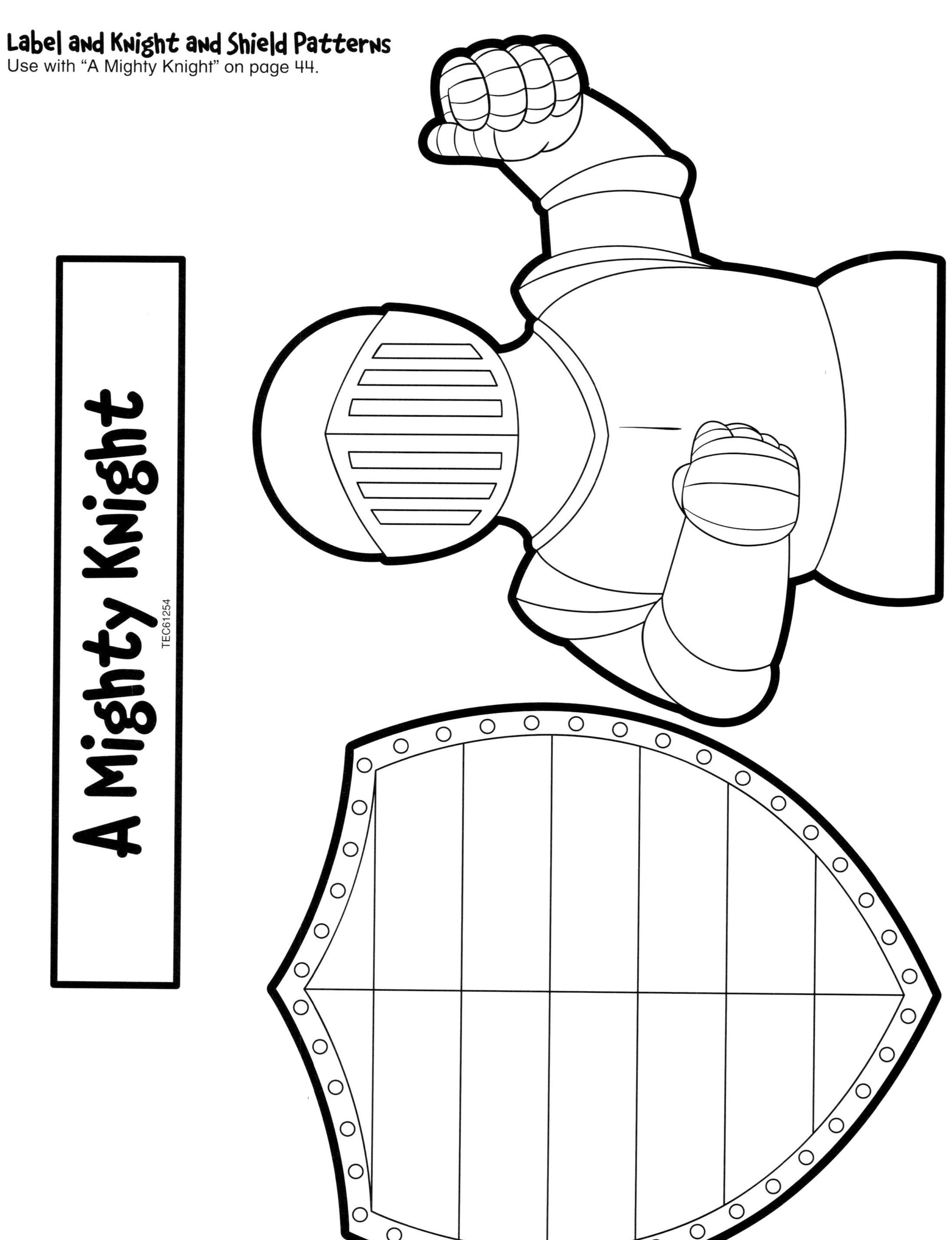

Letter Wheel and Knight Pattern

Use with "Read the Shield" on page 45.

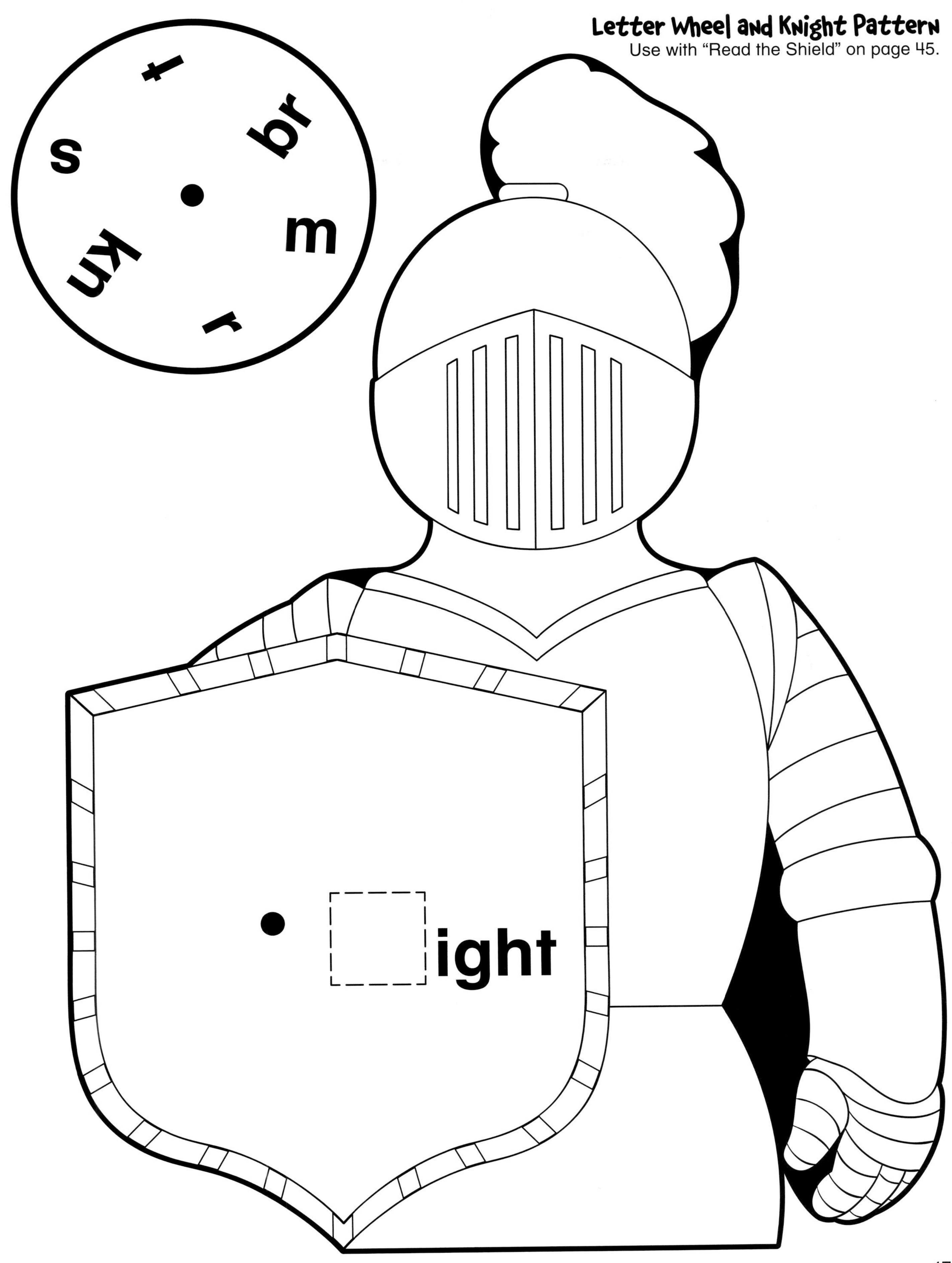

Name ______________________________ *-ight*

A Night Flight

Color the ☆ that makes a real word with **ight**.
Write the word.

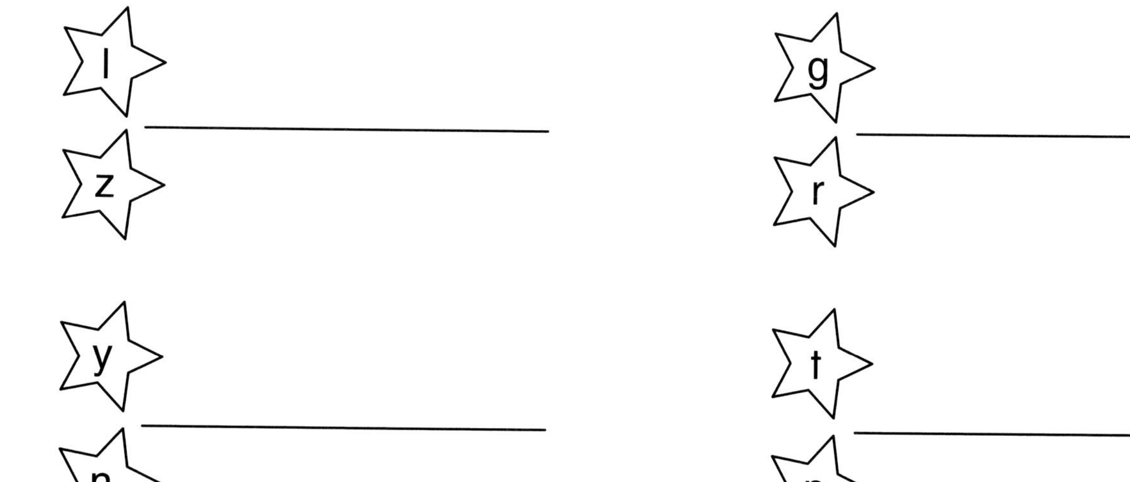

Complete each sentence with a word from above.

1. Please turn off the ______________.
2. I see the moon at ______________.
3. Ouch! Those shoes are too ______________.
4. The sun is so ______________.
5. He holds his pencil in his ______________ hand.

The King of -ing

This *-ing* word family castle is fit for royalty. To begin, have each child write different *-ing* words on eight or more brick patterns copied from page 51.

Materials for one:

completed copy of page 51
9" x 12" sheet of construction paper
construction paper scraps
scissors
glue

Steps:

1. Position the construction paper vertically and trim the top of the paper so it resembles a castle with turrets.
2. Cut out the castle label, king card, and programmed bricks.
3. Glue the label near the bottom of the castle and glue the king card centered above it.
4. Glue the bricks to the castle.
5. Cut a flag from construction paper scraps and glue it in place.

-ing
king
ring
sing
wing

bring
cling
sling
sting
swing
thing

spring
string

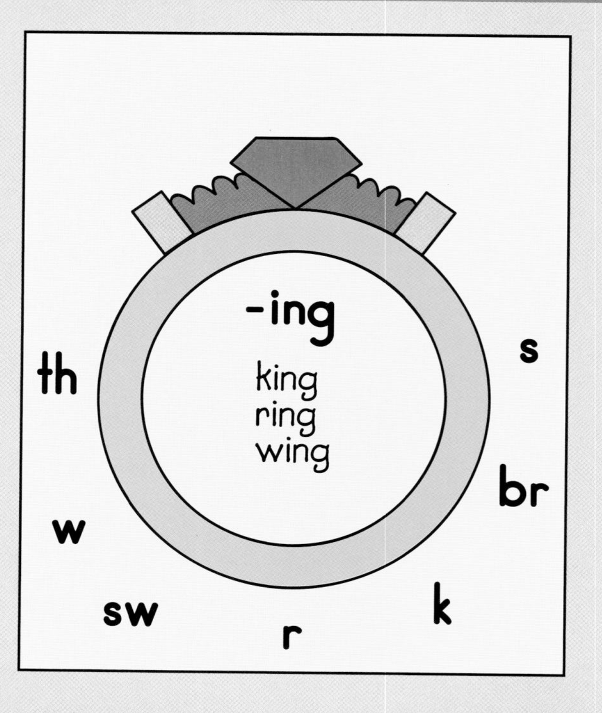

A Remarkable Ring

This large-group activity results in a poster-size reference. Use colorful markers to draw a simple jeweled ring on a large sheet of paper. Write "-ing" inside the ring at the top and then display the poster within student reach. Outside the ring, write onsets that can each be combined with the rime to form a word. Select an onset and have students say the word; then invite a volunteer to write it inside the ring. Continue until all the words you wish to reinforce are written.

Round and Round

For this clever center idea, program the rim of a tagboard circle with onsets that form words when combined with the rime *-ing*. Next, hole-punch one end of a tagboard strip. Poke a brad through the center of the circle and fasten the hole-punched end of the strip to the back. To make a handle, staple a four-inch tagboard square to the other end of the strip near the circle's rim. Then glue a copy of the rime card from page 51 on the square. A student forms words by aligning the rime with an onset on the circle. She reads each word and writes it on her paper. **For a more challenging activity,** include onsets that do not form real words and have students distinguish between real and nonsense words.

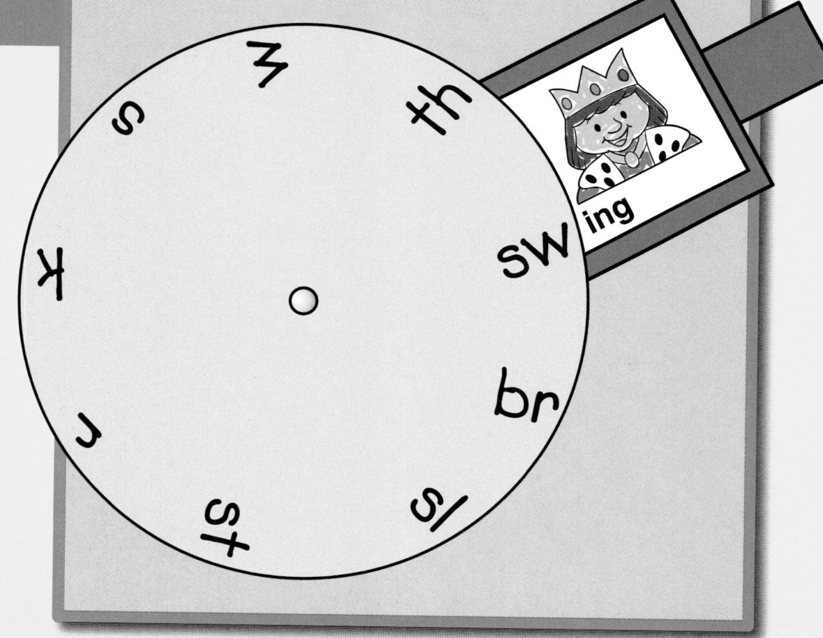

King Card, Castle Label, and Brick Patterns

Use with "The King of *-ing*" on page 49.

Use with "Round and Round" on page 50.

TEC61254

The King of *-ing*

Name ______________________________ -ing

Where Is My Ring?

Write **ing** on each line.
Color each box with a real word.
Read the words on the path to the ring.

	k____	s____	g____
	q____	w____	j____
v____	h____	th____	f____
br____	sl____	sw____	pr____
st____	fr____	pl____	cr____
cl____	str____	r____	

Name ____ *-ing*

A Royal Singer

Write **ing** on each line.

Complete each sentence with a word from above.

1. The king likes to ____________________.
2. Will the bee ____________________ the king?
3. Did the doorbell ____________________?
4. Please ____________________ the mail inside.
5. Kittens like to play with ____________________.
6. Watch the ball and ____________________ the bat.
7. The bird hurt its ____________________.
8. Flowers begin to grow in the ____________________.

-ip

dip
hip
lip
rip
sip
tip
zip

chip
drip
flip
ship
trip

Ship at Sea

This seaworthy vessel is perfect for an *-ip* word family. To begin, have each child write an *-ip* word on each of the rectangles (windows) and each of the circles (portholes) on a copy of page 56.

Materials for one:

completed copy of page 56
9" x 12" sheet of blue construction paper
scissors
glue

Steps:

1. Position the construction paper horizontally and then fold up the bottom 1½ inches. Then cut wave lines across the top edge of the folded flap. Put a drop of glue inside each end so the waves make a pocket for the ship.
2. Cut out the ship label and the ship.
3. Glue the label on the waves.
4. Slide the ship behind the waves.

The *-ip* Clip

To prepare for this hands-on activity, label each two-inch card in a set with a different onset that makes a word with the *-ip* rime. Place the cards in a container. Write "____ip" on an index card, leaving room for an onset card.

During small-group time, a child takes an onset card, clips it to the programmed index card, and reads the word aloud. Then each group member writes the word on a sheet of paper. After all students have finished writing, the child shows the card to the group for them to check their spellings. To play again, remove the onset card and have another child repeat the activity.

A Ship Flipbook

The result of this activity is a ready-to-go review of an *-ip* word family. To make a flipbook, a child colors and cuts out the ship flipbook pattern and letter cards on a copy of page 57. He stacks the cards behind the *sh* card, places them atop the letter *z* on the ship, and staples them in place. Then he flips the letter cards to read each *-ip* word. **For a more advanced version,** have him write each word and a few of his own on a sheet of paper to form an *-ip* word family.

Ship Label and Ship Pattern

Use with "Ship at Sea" on page 54.

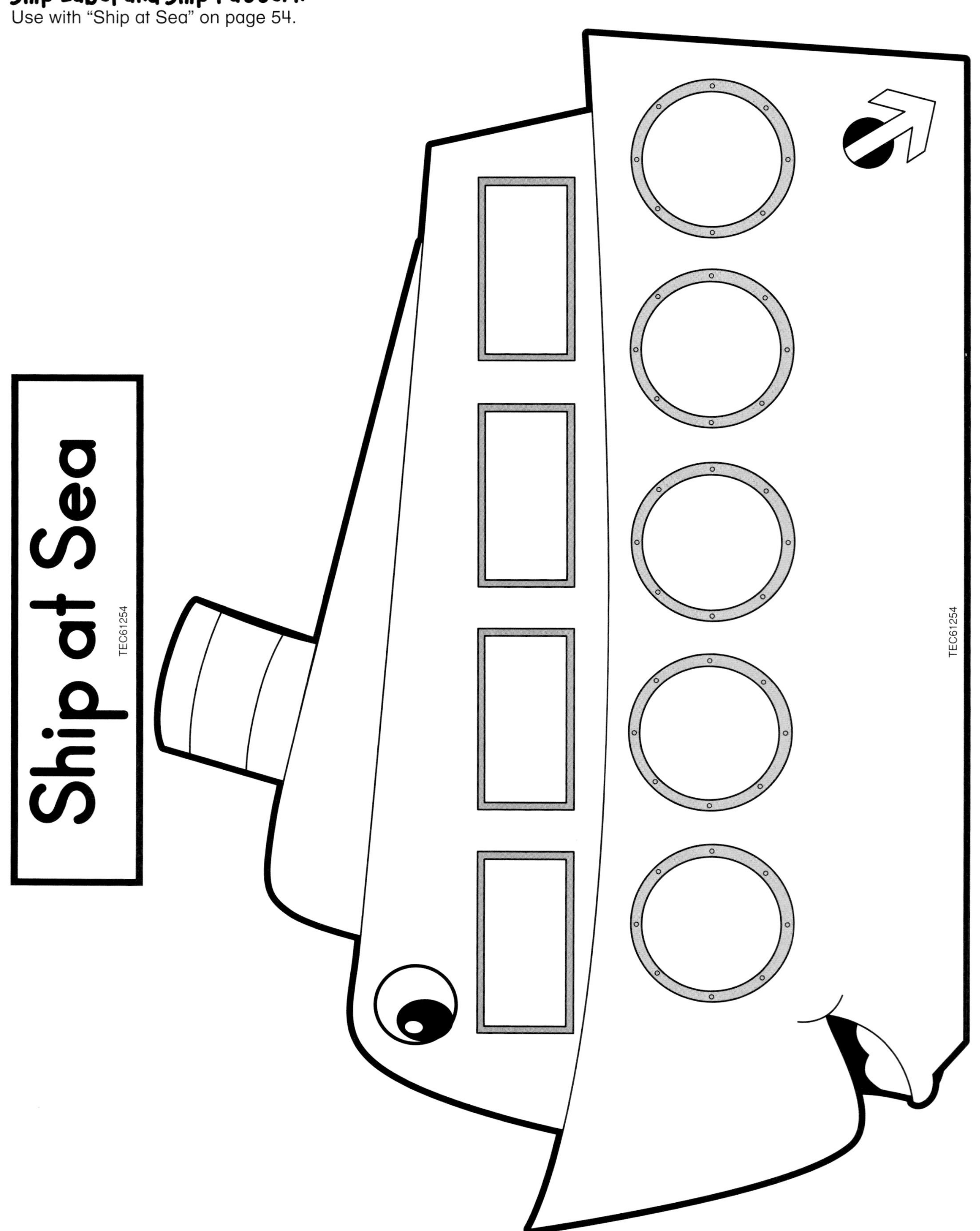

Ship Flipbook Pattern and Letter Cards

Use with "A Ship Flipbook" on page 55.

Name ________________________________ *-ip*

Hippo Dip

Write the word for each picture.
Use the word bank.

Complete each sentence with a word from above.

1. Have you ever been on a big ________________?
2. Did you eat the last ________________?
3. Let me ________________ up my jacket.
4. I did not mean to ________________ my paper.

-ock

Ticktock Clock

Have students make this cuckoo clock to practice spelling, reading, and writing *-ock* words.

Materials for one:

clock pattern (page 61)
two 1" x 3" paper strips
1" x 12" paper strip
2 paper circles
writing paper
scissors
glue

Steps:

1. Cut out the clock.
2. Glue one 1" x 3" strip to the bottom right of the clock. Write "ock" on a circle and glue it to the bottom of the secured strip.
3. Glue the left and right edges of the other 1" x 3" strip to the back of the clock, as shown.
4. Glue the remaining circle to one end of the 1" x 12" strip. Then slide the opposite end of the strip through the small strip from Step 3.
5. Pull the left strip down and write different onsets that form real words when paired with *-ock*.
6. Write your words on a separate sheet of paper to form an *-ock* word family.

-ock

dock
lock
mock
rock
sock

block
clock
flock
knock
shock
smock
stock

Left Sock, Right Sock

To prepare for this center activity, make several pairs of sock cutouts. On each left sock, write an onset that forms a real word when coupled with the rime *-ock*. Then write "ock" on each right sock. Store the socks and writing paper in a laundry basket at a center.

A child sorts the socks into pairs to make *-ock* words. Then he writes "-ock" at the top of a sheet of paper and copies the words to form a word family.

Words Around the Clock

This *-ock* word family clock is the perfect tool for a quick assessment. To begin, help youngsters read the *-ock* word cards on a copy of page 62. Then have each child cut out the clock patterns. Have him glue the word cards on the clockface and attach the hands with a brad.

To assess individual students' progress in a group setting, name two *-ock* words on the clock and direct each child to use the hands to point to each word. Since the clocks are likely to be different, each student must focus on her own clock to find each word!

Use with "Ticktock Clock" on page 59.

Clock Patterns and Word Cards

Use with "Words Around the Clock" on page 60.

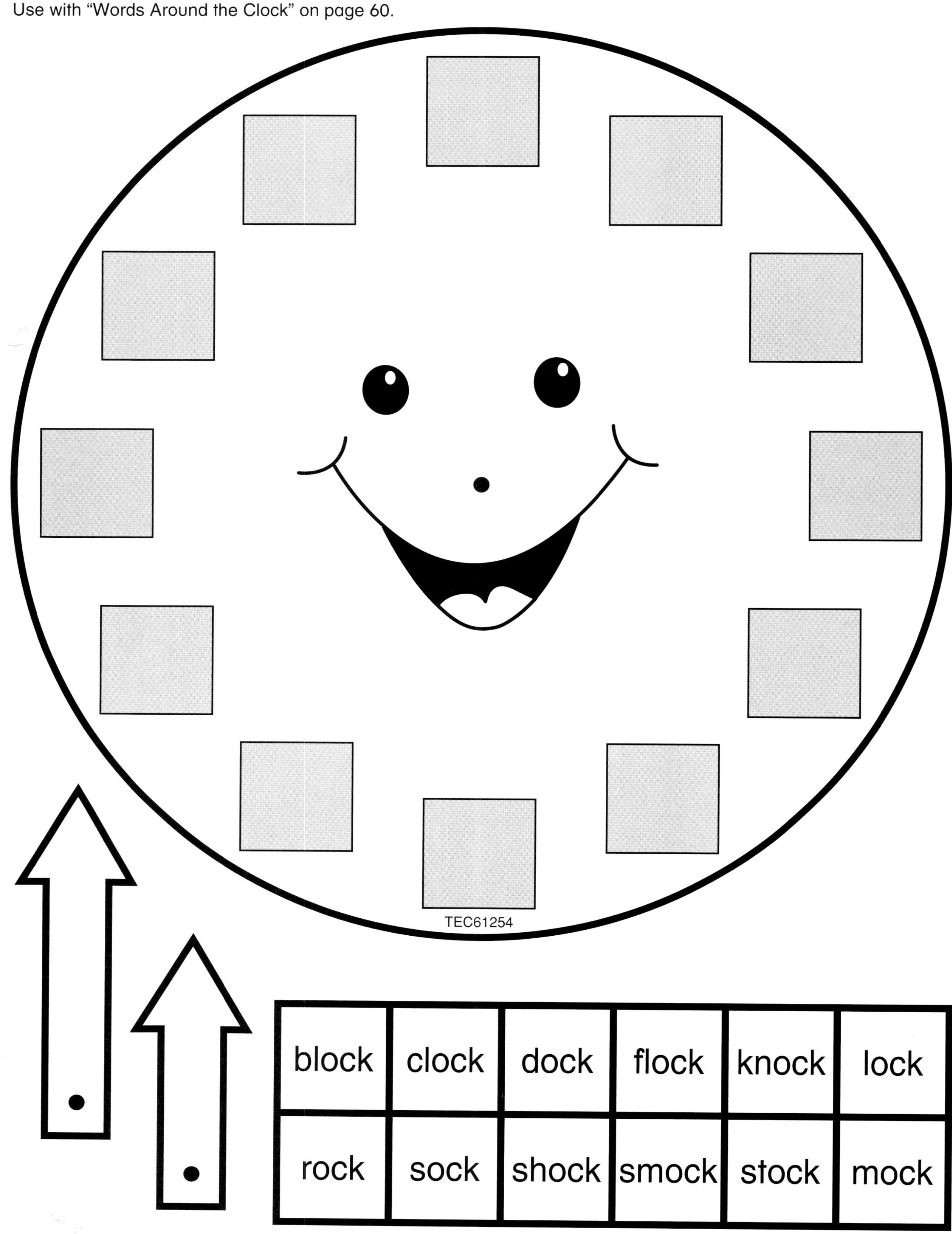

block	clock	dock	flock	knock	lock
rock	sock	shock	smock	stock	mock

Name ____________________ *-ock*

Block Climbers

Write **ock** to complete each word.
Cut. Glue to match.

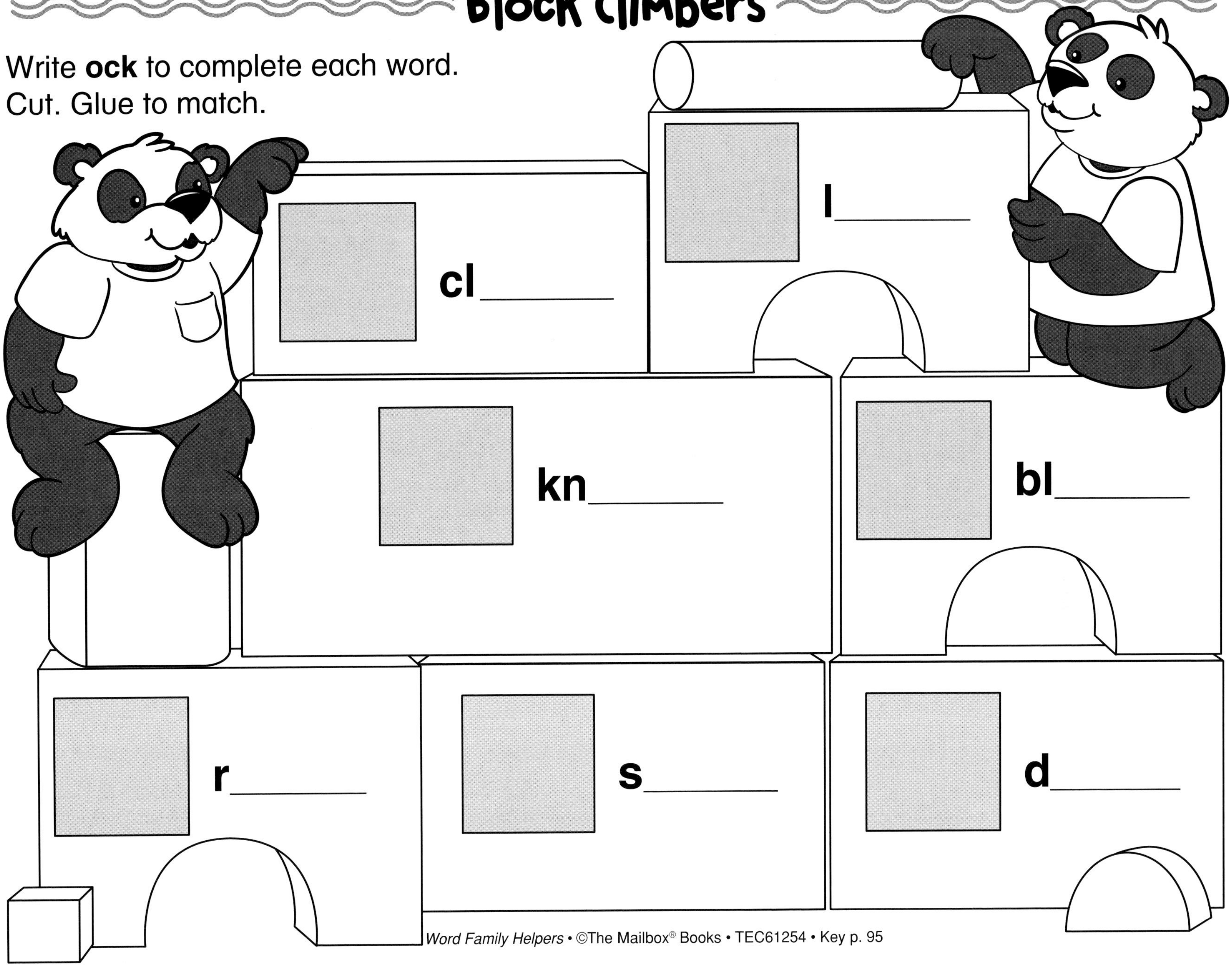

cl______

l______

kn______

bl______

r______

s______

d______

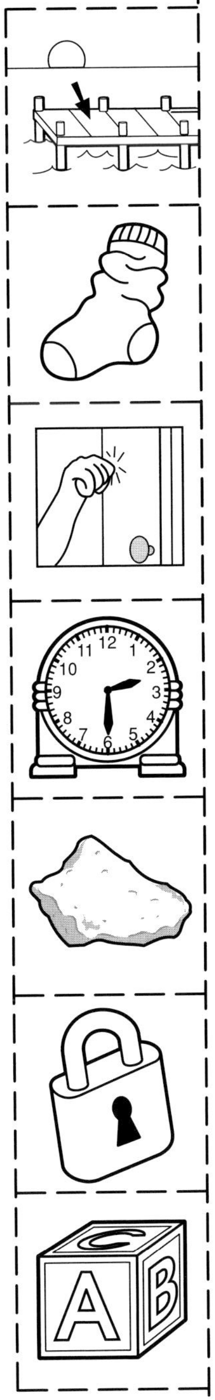

-op

cop
hop
mop
pop
top

chop
drop
flop
plop
prop
shop
stop

The Top Mop

When a child finishes this project, have him use the mop as a pointer to "mop up" each *-op* word as he reads it.

Materials for one:

label, bucket, and mop patterns (page 66)
6" x 9" construction paper
craft stick
crayons
scissors
glue

Steps:

1. Color and cut out the label, bucket, and mop patterns.
2. Glue the label near the top of the construction paper.
3. Below the label, glue the left, right, and bottom edges of the bucket to make a pocket. Then draw a handle on the bucket.
4. Write eight to ten *-op* words on the construction paper; then use a blue crayon to draw a puddle around each word.
5. To make the mop pointer, glue the mop cutout to the craft stick. When the glue is dry, store the mop in the bucket.

Time to Shop!

Take your students shopping for *-op* words with this small-group activity. In advance, place *-op* word items—such as a mop, top, stop sign, and flip-flop—in various classroom locations. Carry a shopping bag and take the group around the room to "shop" for items in the *-op* word family. Randomly hold up an item and have a student name it. If the word ends with *-op,* place the item in the shopping bag; if not, return the item to its original location.

Stop to Read

The student-made booklets at this center provide practice reading *-op* words. For each child, set out a copy of the booklet backing and booklet page from page 66, a copy of page 67, and a jumbo craft stick. Also provide a red crayon, scissors, tape, and a stapler. A child colors the booklet backing and pages and cuts them out. Then she stacks the pages on the left side of the booklet backing and staples them together. Finally, she tapes a jumbo craft stick to the back of the booklet for a handle.

Label, Bucket, and Mop Patterns

Use with "The Top Mop" on page 64.

The Top Mop

TEC61254

Booklet Backing and Booklet Page

Use with "Stop to Read" on page 65.

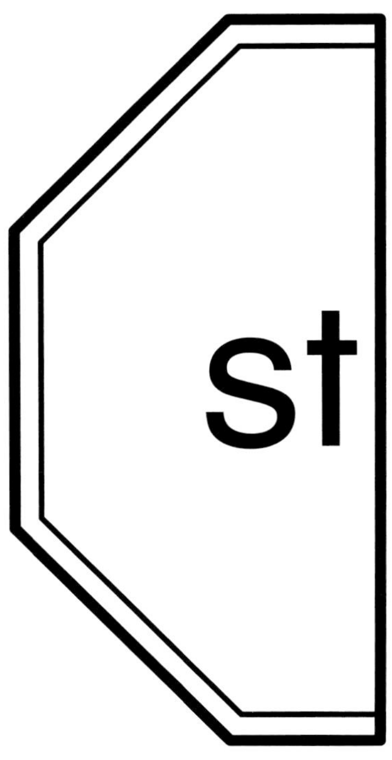

Use with "Stop to Read" on page 65.

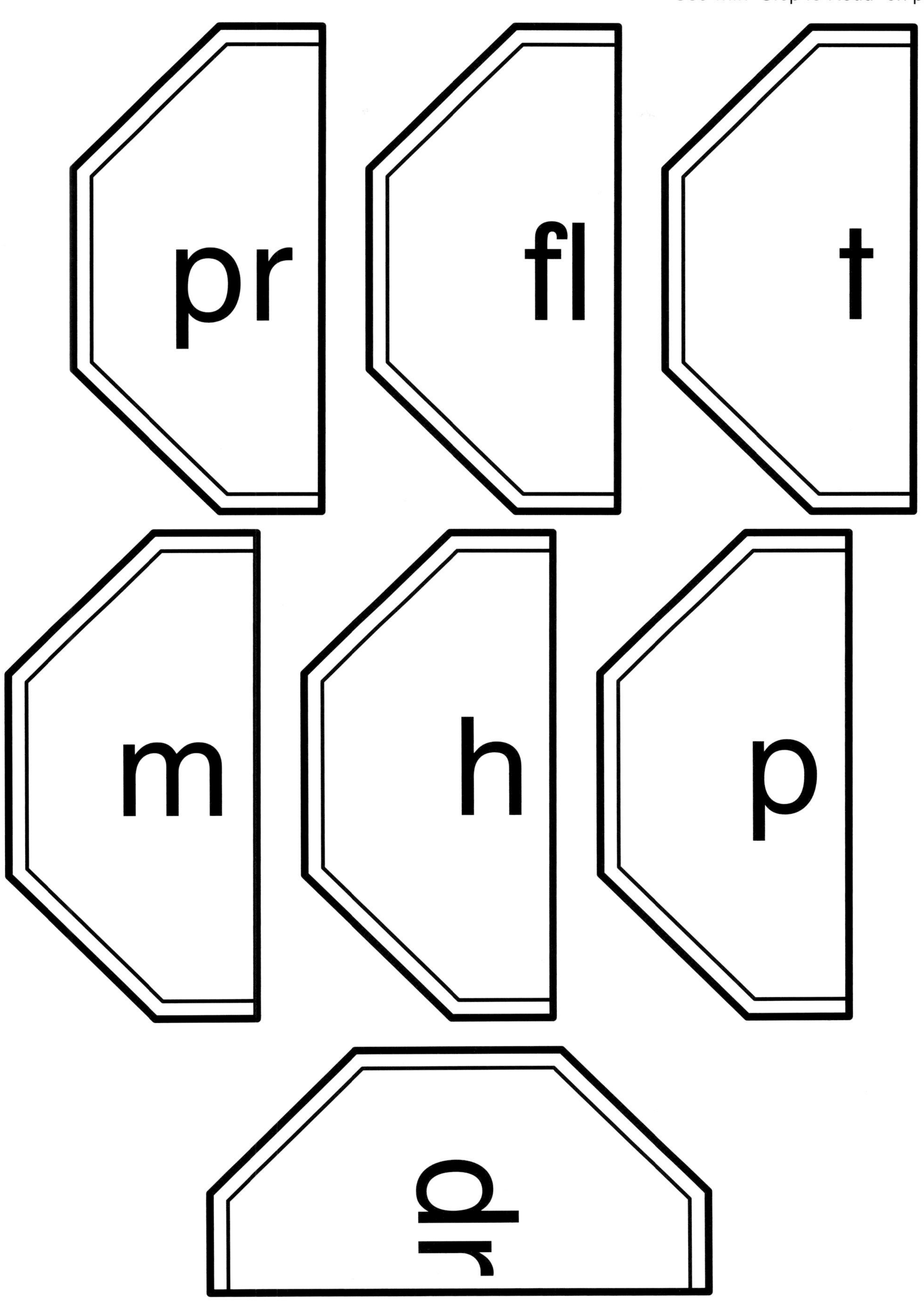

Name ____________________

Pop! Pop! Pop!

Color each popcorn piece that makes a real **op** word.
Write the words.

n p t
dr
m
h d
sh st
y
pl

______op ______op

______op ______op

______op ______op

______op ______op

Ice Cream Truck

Students review the *-uck* word family with this cool cargo. To begin, have each child read the words on a copy of page 71. Instruct her to color the ice cream cards that have *-uck* words. Then have her write her name on the truck label and draw herself in the window.

Materials for one:

completed copy of page 71
9" x 12" sheet of construction paper
2 construction paper circles (wheels)
2 brads
scissors
glue

Steps:

1. Cut out the truck label and the ice cream cards. Discard the noncolored cards.
2. Position the paper horizontally and glue the label to the top right. Then cut the top left corner of the paper, as shown, to make a truck shape.
3. Use the brads to attach the wheels to the truck.
4. Glue each ice cream card to the truck.

-uck

buck
duck
luck
muck
puck
suck
tuck

cluck
pluck
stuck
truck

struck

Lucky Duck!

Inspire youngsters to review *-uck* words with these three- and four-leaf clovers! Write different words that end with *-uck* on copies of the clover cards on page 72. Place the cards in a bag.

Students pass the bag around the group-time circle, singing the song shown. When they sing the word *stop* in Line 5, the player holding the bag stands until the song's end. Then she removes a card and reads it aloud. If the word is written on a four-leaf clover, she is a lucky duck and gets to waddle around the circle while chanting, "Uck!" Continue as time allows.

(sung to the tune of "Are You Sleeping?")
Pass the *-uck* words.
Pass the *-uck* words
Round and round,
Round and round.
Stop the bag; don't look inside.
When it's time, *-uck* is your guide.
Read the word.
Read the word.

A Stuck Truck

For this *-uck* word family review, have each child lightly color and cut out a copy of the truck pattern and onset strip on page 72. Instruct him to glue the truck to a sheet of construction paper and add mud details. When the glue is dry, help him cut slits where indicated and thread the onset strip through the slits to form words. For a follow-up activity, have each child write his *-uck* words on cloud cutouts and glue them to the project.

Use with "Ice Cream Truck" on page 69.

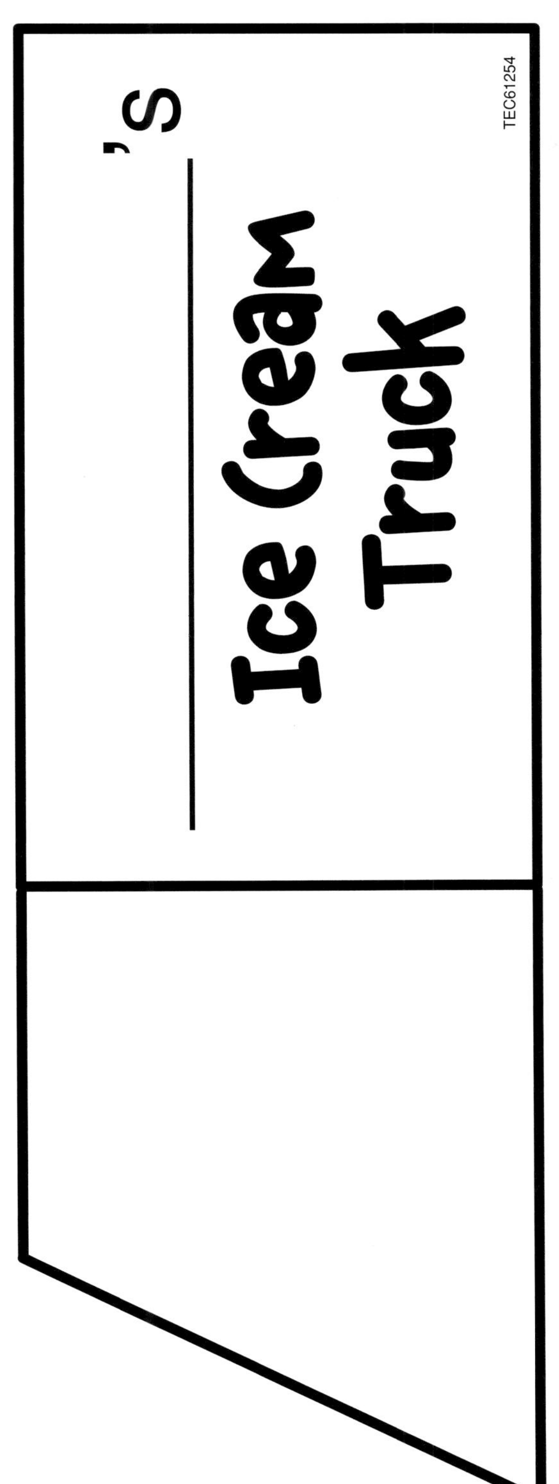

Clover Cards

Use with "Lucky Duck!" on page 70.

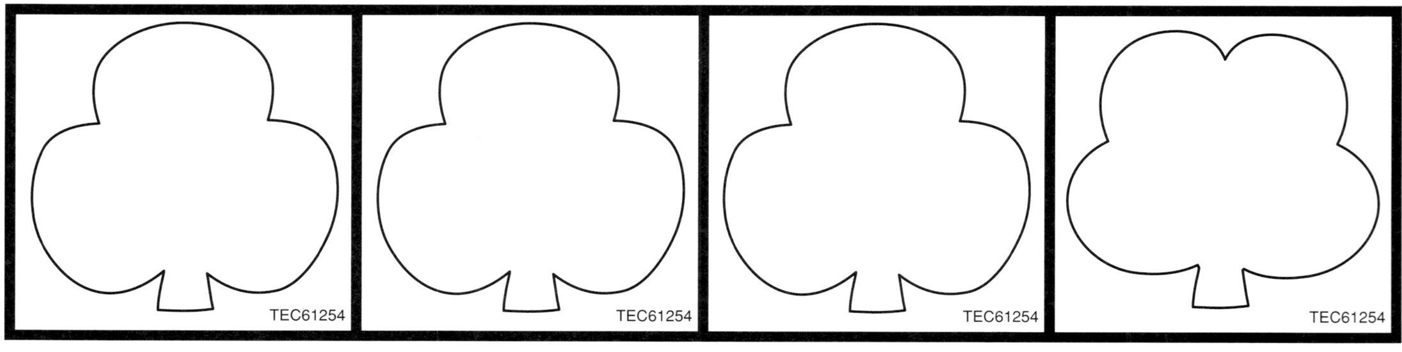

Truck Pattern and Onset Strip

Use with "A Stuck Truck" on page 70.

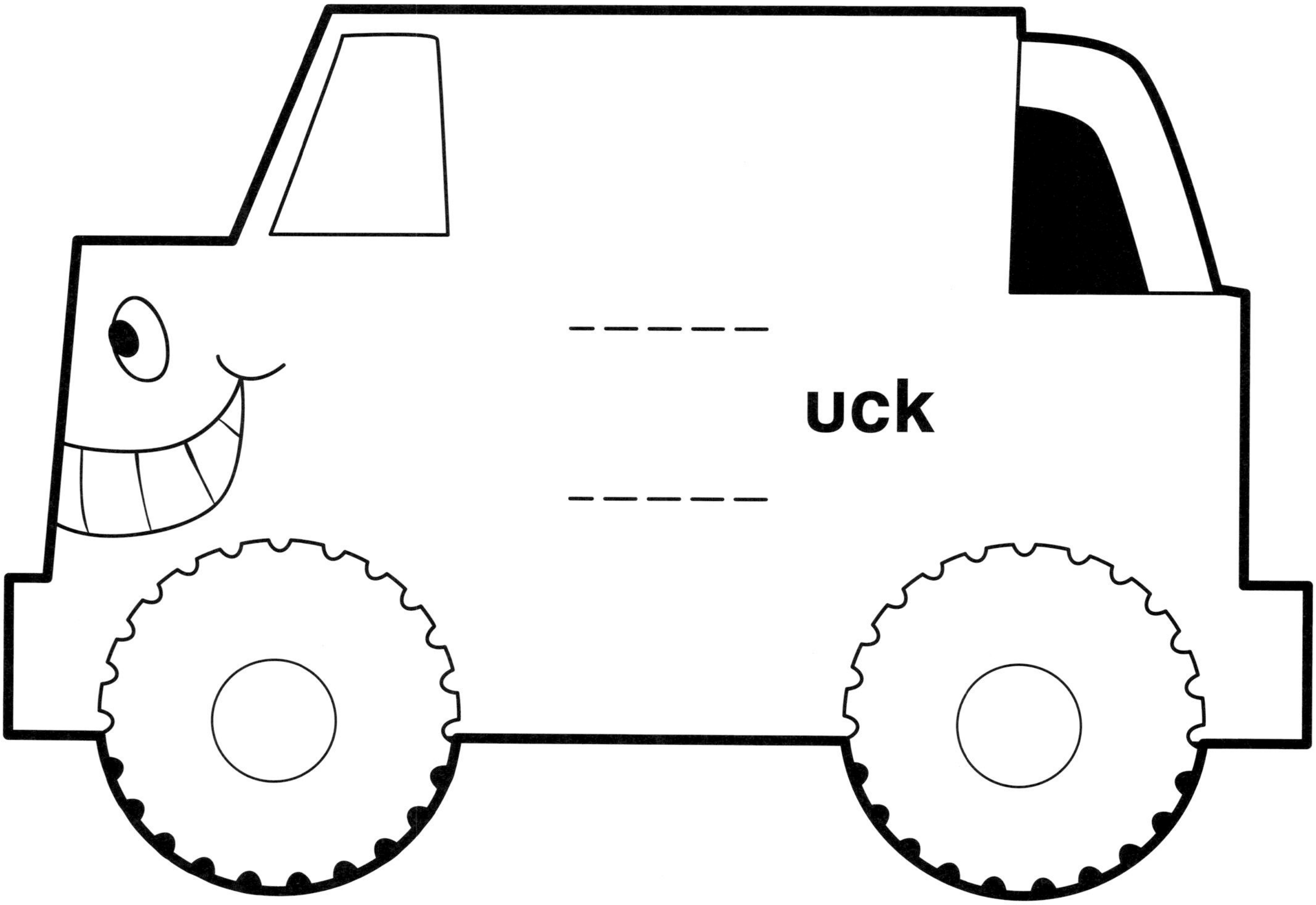

uck

t	d	l	p	tr	pl	cl	TEC61254

Name ____________________

A Path for Duck

Read each word.
Color the **uck** words.

best	lick	puck	duck	cluck		
say	ring	luck	flap	sick	bump	sip
		stuck	truck	buck	muck	hop
		cup	zip	nest	tuck	rock
		struck	yuck	pluck	suck	play

Quacker Crackers

-ump

bump
dump
hump
jump
lump
pump

clump
grump
plump
slump
stump
thump

Stump Jump

After making this 3-D project, have each child make his beaver "jump" from log to log and over the stumps as he reads the *-ump* words. To begin, have each child write a different *-ump* word on each log on a tan copy of page 76.

Materials for one:

completed copy of page 76
4½" x 24" green construction paper strip
three 1½" x 6" brown construction paper strips
scissors
glue

Steps:

1. Cut out the logs, the beaver card, and the label.
2. Fold the beaver card along the thin fold lines; then glue to secure the card as shown.
3. Glue the label near the bottom of the vertically aligned construction paper.
4. Glue the ends of each brown strip together to make three rings. Then cut slits along one side of each ring and fold up the resulting tabs to make a stump.
5. Glue the stumps and the logs to the green paper as shown.

Jump for -ump

This small-group activity helps students recognize *-ump* words. Program a set of cards with some words in the *-ump* word family and some in other word families. To begin, gather youngsters in an open area. Hold up a word card and have a volunteer read the word aloud. If the word contains the rime *-ump,* each child jumps and says, "Ump!" If the word does not contain the rime *-ump,* each child remains still.

Stump Your Students

To begin this class game, secretly choose an *-ump* word. Tell students that you are going to try to stump them and then announce a clue that describes the word. Next, have each student write his guess on a sheet of paper. Remind youngsters that the word should contain the rime *-ump*. Ask a volunteer to announce his answer and have the other students check their answers. Continue play with other *-ump* words.

Label, Beaver Card, and Log Patterns

Use with "Stump Jump" on page 74.

Stump Jump

TEC61254

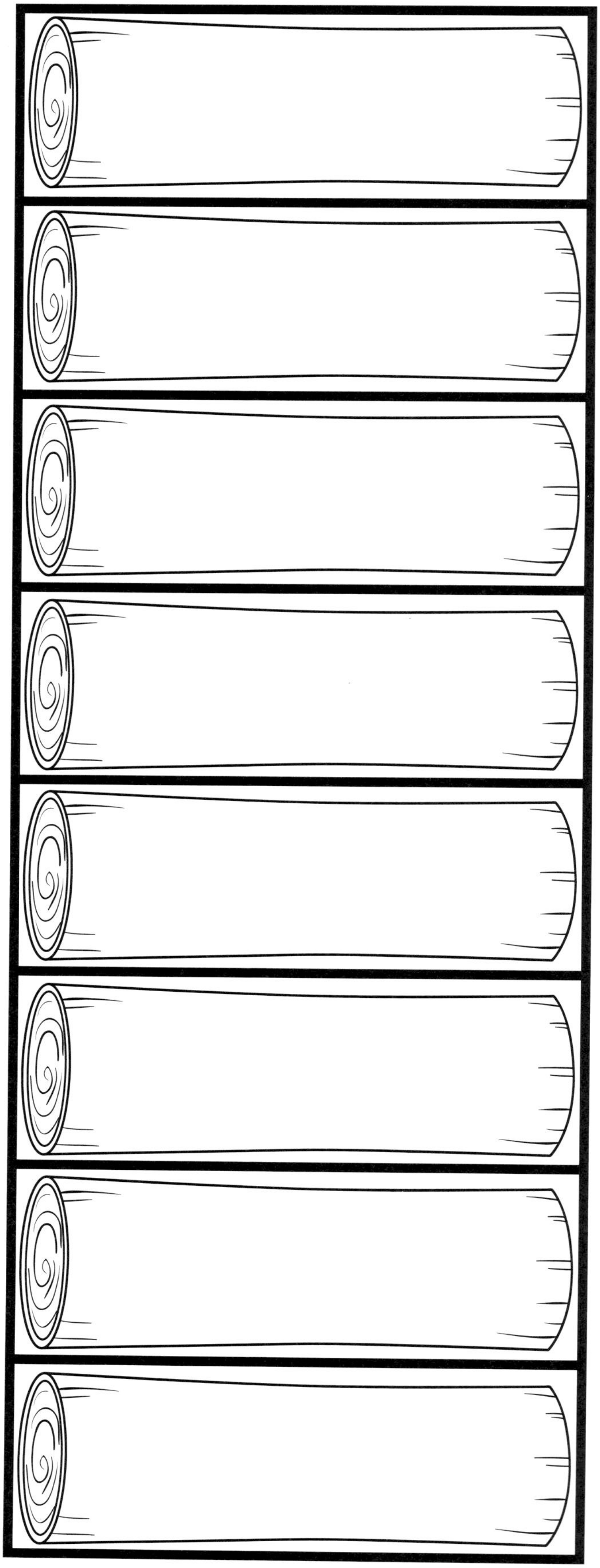

Name ____________________

At the Pump

Color the words in the **ump** word family.

Write each **ump** word.

1. ____________________

2. ____________________

3. ____________________

4. ____________________

5. ____________________

6. ____________________

Name ______________________________ -ump

Thump, Thump, Thump!

Write the word to match each picture.
Use the word bank.

Word Bank

bump pump hump
jump stump dump

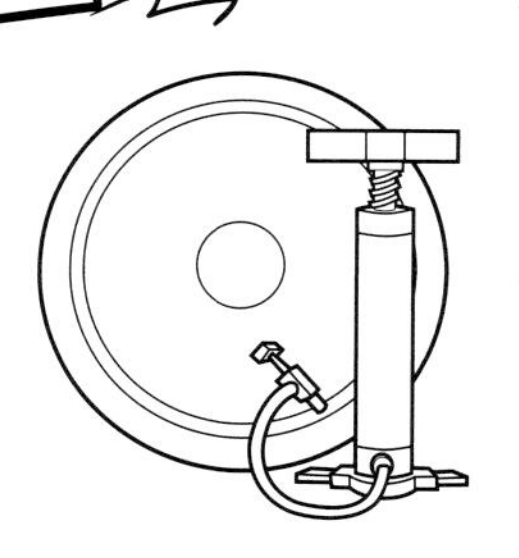

______________ ______________ ______________

______________ ______________ ______________

Complete each sentence with a word from above.

1. I sat on a tree ______________.
2. That camel only has one ______________.
3. I am going to ______________ this dirt in the garden.
4. How high can you ______________?
5. That is a big ______________ on your head!
6. Use the ______________ to put air in your tires.

Name ______________________

Bedtime Story

Write **ack** or **ick** to complete each word.
Cut. Glue to match.

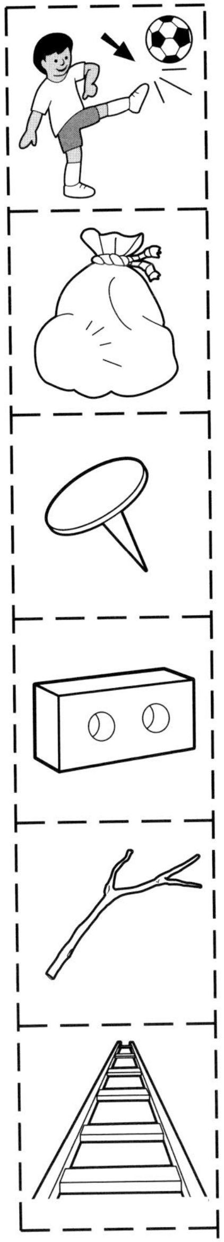

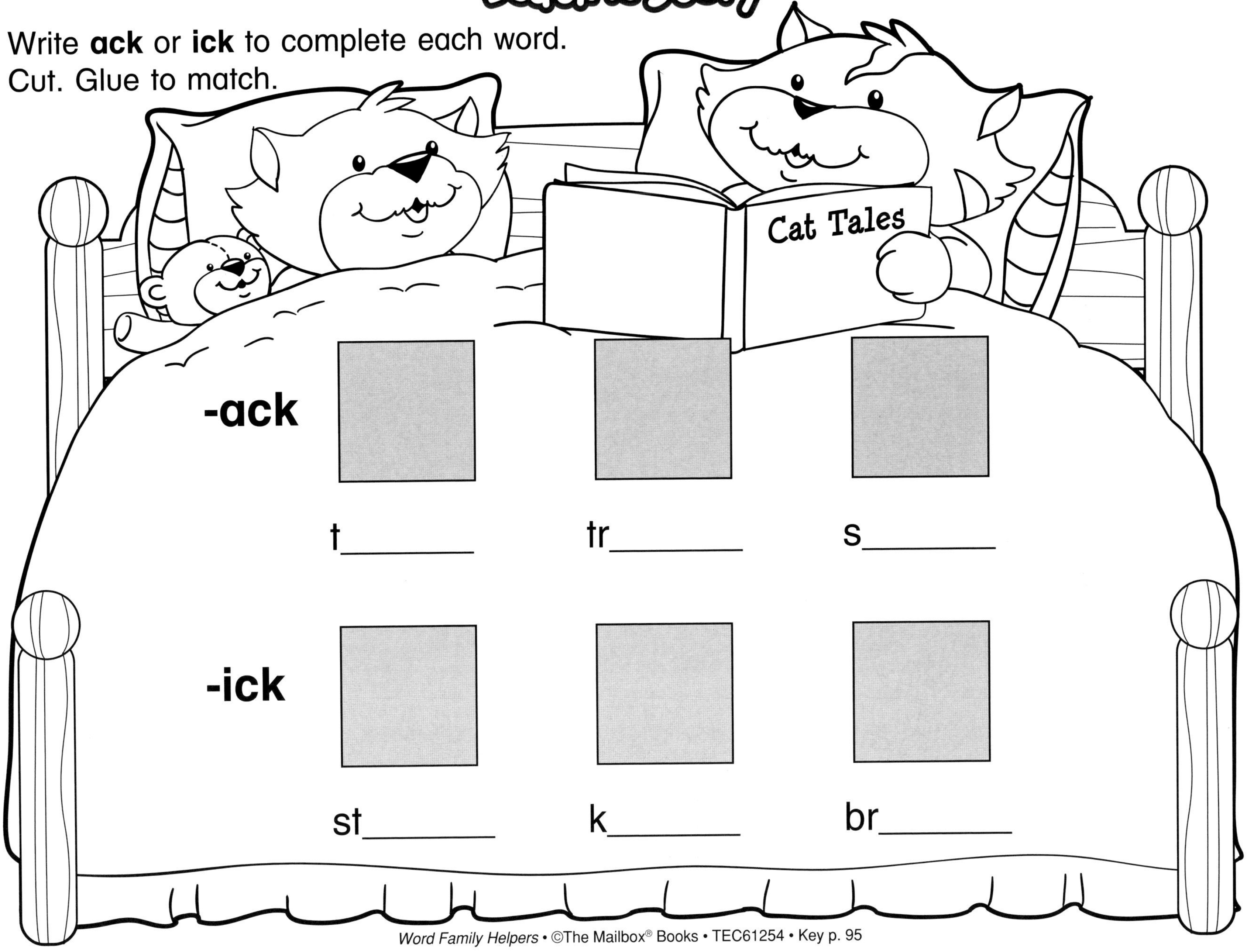

Cat Tales

-ack

t_______ tr_______ s_______

-ick

st_______ k_______ br_______

Name ____________________

Buzzing By

Write the word for each picture.
Use the word bank to help you.

Farm Dancing

Complete each sentence.
Use the word bank.

Word Bank

-ack	**-ick**	**-ock**	**-uck**
quack	chick	clock	truck
back	pick	knock	luck

1. What time does the ______________ say?
2. Good ______________ finding your lost dog.
3. When will you get ______________ home?
4. I think I heard a ______________ at the door.
5. My dad drives a big ______________.
6. A baby ______________ just hatched.
7. Please ______________ up your toys.
8. That duck made a very loud ______________.

Name ______________________________

Buckets of Fun

Write the word for each picture.
Use the word bank.

Complete each sentence with a word from above.

1. Let's ______________ the leaves together.
2. Did you read the ______________ yet?
3. His boat has a red ______________.
4. Blow the candles out on your ______________.
5. I will have a vanilla ______________, please.
6. The ______________ has a pretty shell.

Name ______________________________

Mission Complete

Color by the code.
Read the words in each word family.

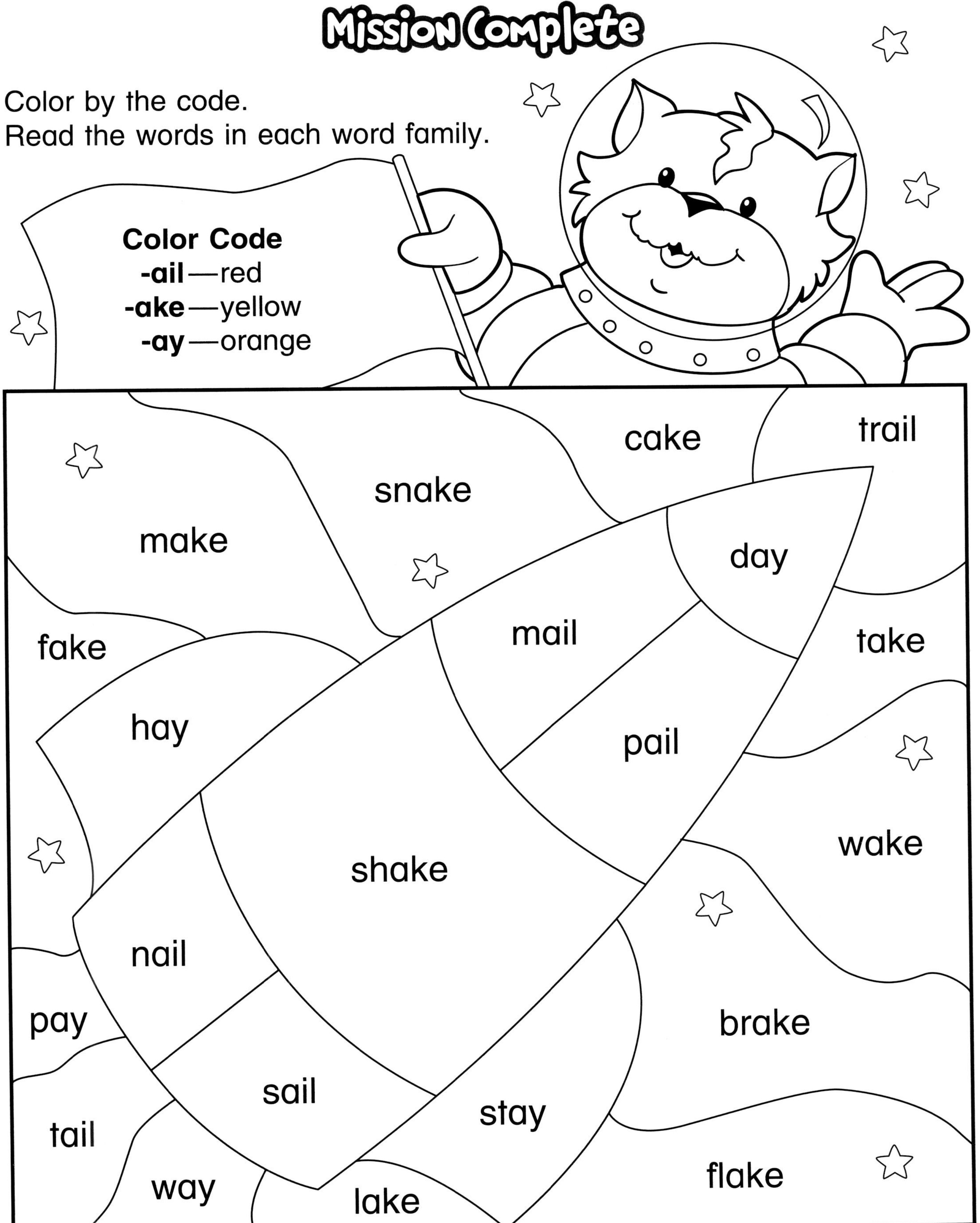

Name______________________________

Teddy Bear Picnic

Write the words to match the pictures in each word family.
Cross out the beginning letter or letters as you use them.

b
c
n
r
l
m
cl
sn

-ap

____

____

____

____

-ake

____

____

____

____

Name ________________________________ *-ake, -ap, -ay*

Fishing for Lunch

Color by the code.

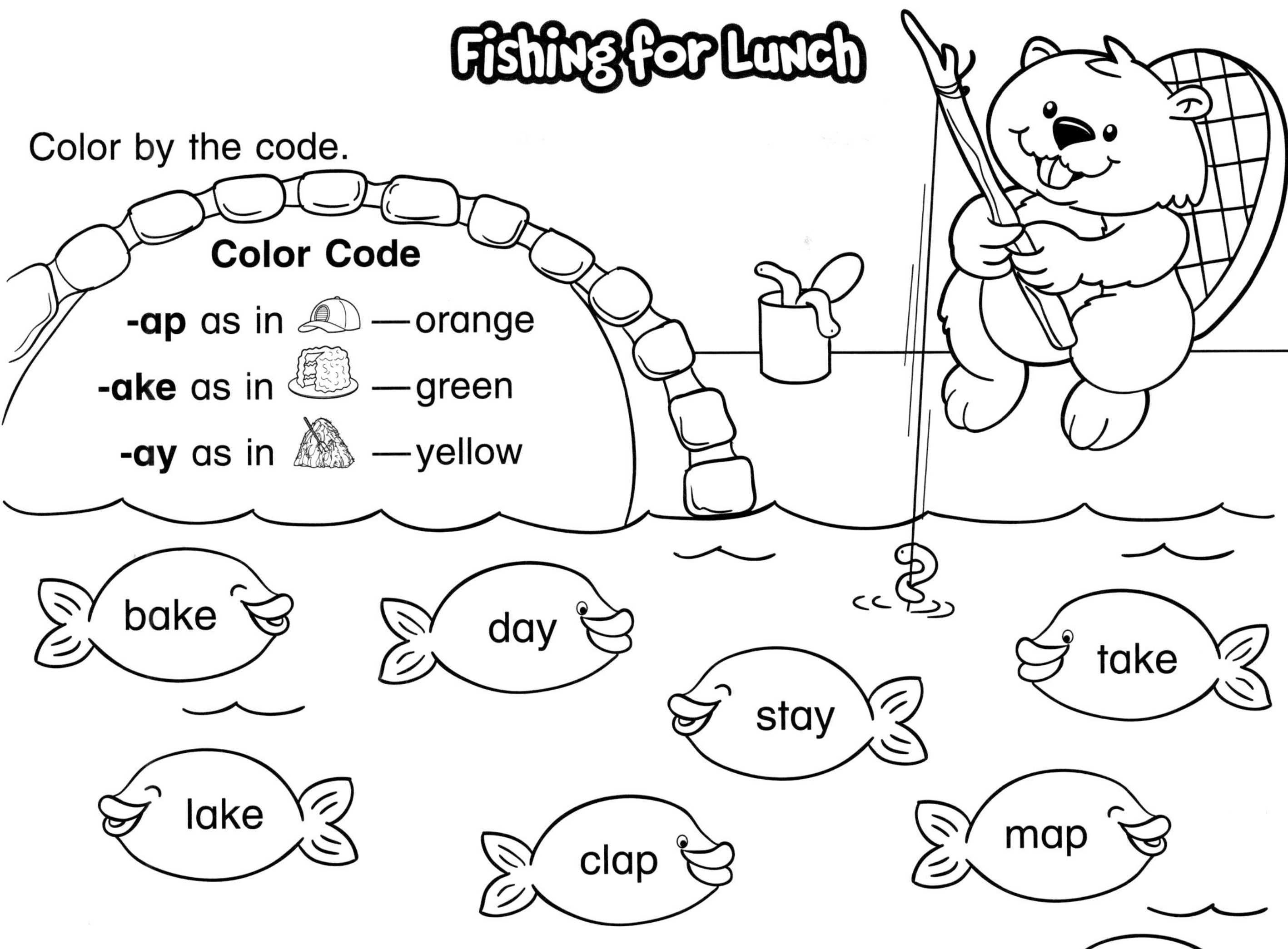

Complete each sentence with a word from above.

1. I will use the ____________________ to find my way.
2. Would you like to ____________________ for lunch?
3. My mom will ____________________ you home.
4. Let's ____________________ our hands together.
5. It's a great ____________________ to be outside.
6. There were many boats on the ____________________.
7. The fat cat fell asleep on my ____________________.
8. Did you ____________________ cookies?

Name ____________________ *-ap, -ip*

Pizza, Anyone?

Write each word below the matching word ending.
Color by the code.

Color Code

-ap as in (cap)—yellow **-ip** as in (ship)—red

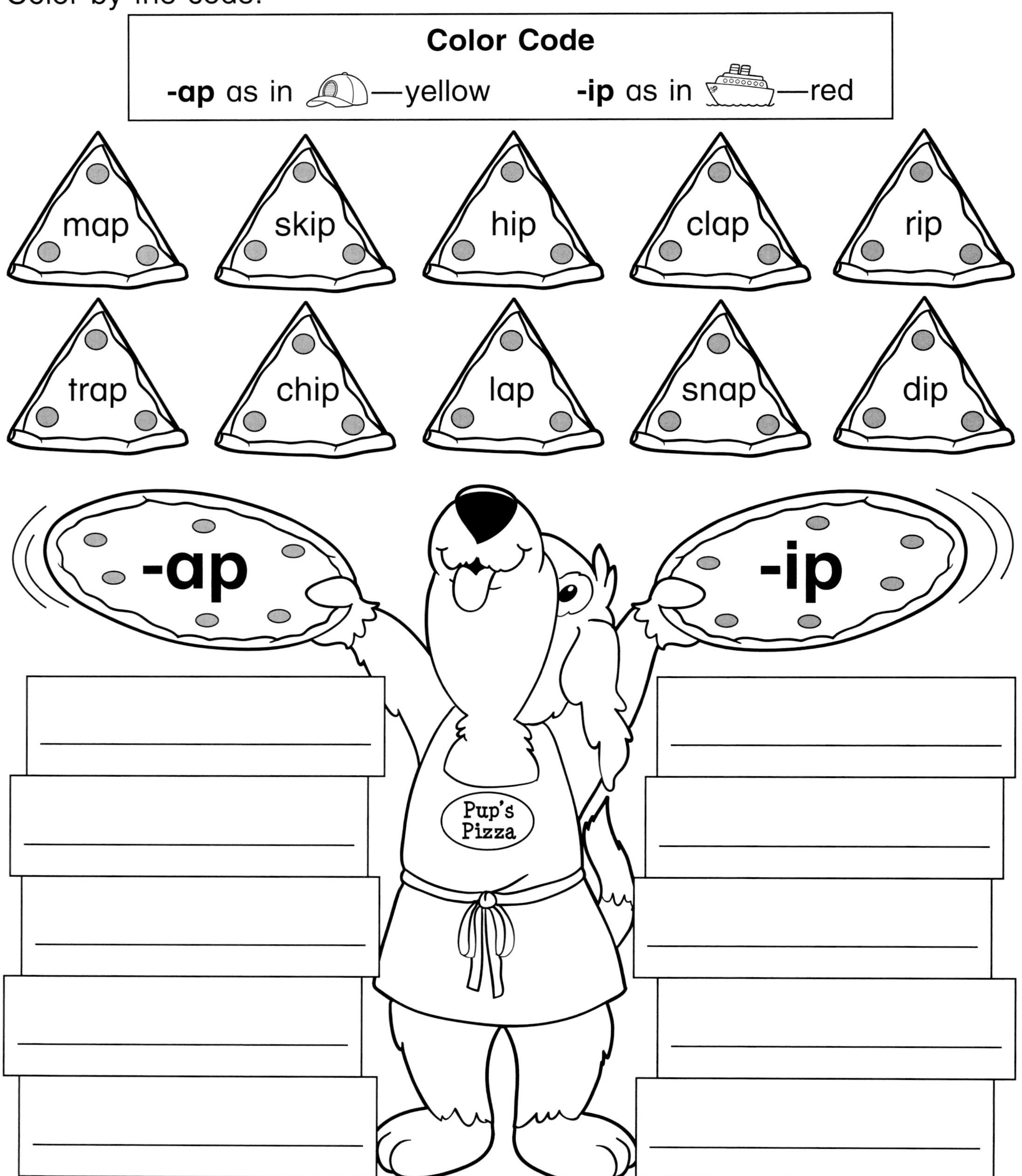

Name______________________

Prizewinning Quilt

Cut.
Glue to match.

-ap	-ip	-op
cap	rip	top
map	lip	mop
nap	ship	pop

Name______________________________

Three in a Row

Circle each word with the matching word ending.
Write the circled words to make word families.

-ed

bed	dot	zip
lap	red	get
hen	net	shed

-ell

pal	tell	wet
cot	fell	pup
tap	yell	hop

-eat

day	mop	yet
neat	beat	heat
hip	let	nut

-ed

____

____

____

-ell

____

____

____

-eat

____

____

____

Name ____

Balancing Act

Color the **et** balls yellow.
Color the **est** balls orange.
Cut. Glue to match.

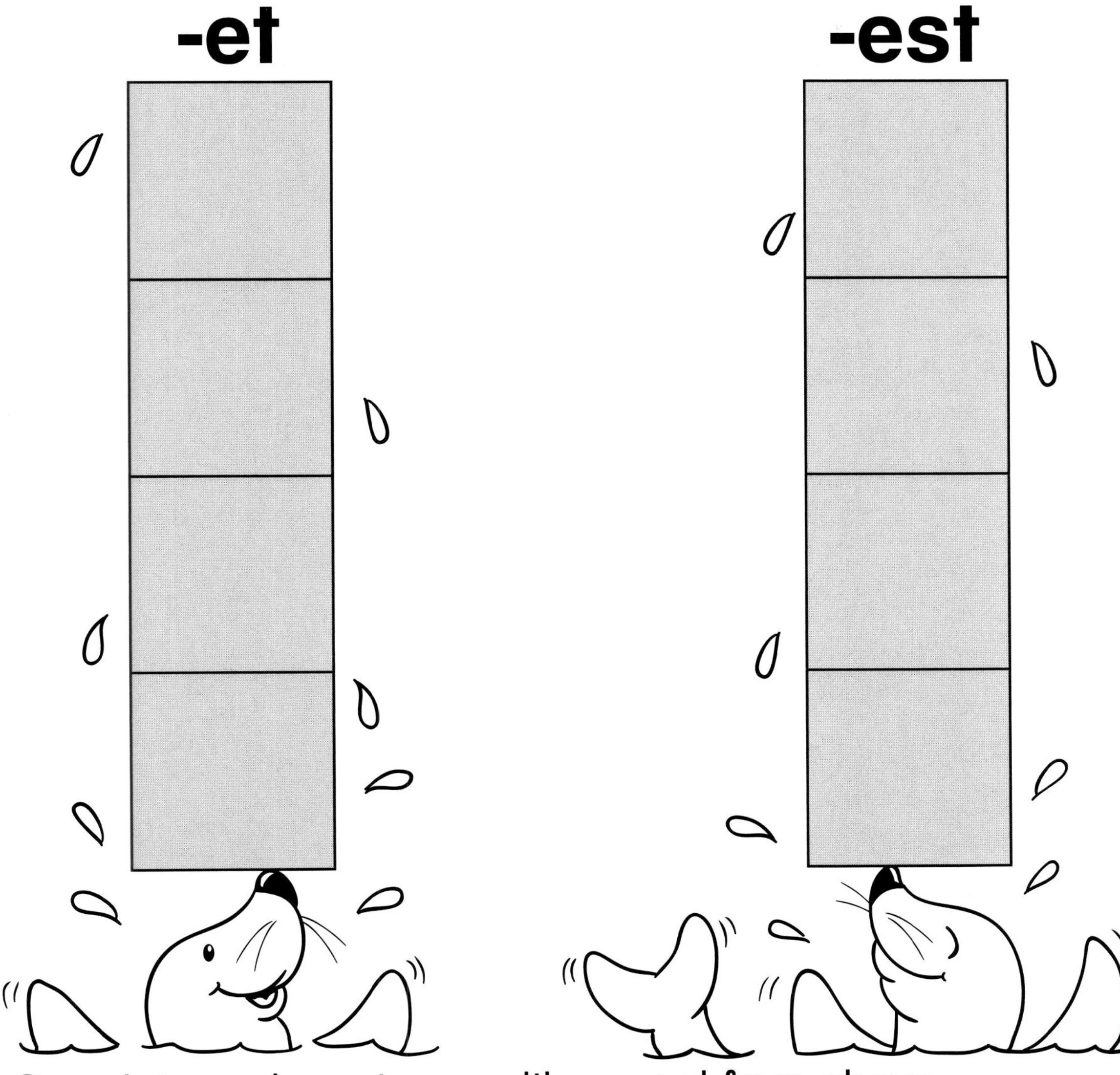

get
rest
pet
let
west
pest
met
best

Complete each sentence with a word from above.

1. Tom ____________________ me for lunch.
2. My ____________________ dog is named Max.
3. We are ____________________ friends.
4. This little fly is being a ____________________.
5. I am going to ____________________ on the bed.

Name______________________

Treetop Stop

Circle the real words.
Write the real words below.

bright pight tight might
light sight vight
dight fright jight

-ight

bint hint squint print
mint yint chint
lint drint sprint

-int

Name ____

Dino Days

Write **ip, ick,** or **ing** to complete each word.
Circle the words in the puzzle below.

h	a	o	t	m	l	i	c	k
i	s	x	h	b	r	i	n	g
p	w	u	i	c	d	r	i	p
o	i	e	c	w	a	o	t	e
b	n	r	k	m	p	i	c	k
l	g	j	s	i	n	g	x	u
e	r	m	f	l	i	p	z	o

All in Bloom

Draw an orange around each **op** word.
Draw a yellow around each **ock** word.

drop lock top shop clock rock sock pop

Write each word below the matching word ending.

-op	**-ock**
________	________
________	________
________	________
________	________

Name ____________________

Bumper Cars

Cut. Glue to match **uck** or **ump.**

-uck

-ump

duck
tuck
jump
pump
stuck
bump

Complete each sentence with a word from above.

1. That ______________ lost a feather.
2. I can ______________ over the puddle.
3. How did you get that ______________ on your head?
4. My mom will ______________ me into bed.
5. You need to ______________ air in your tire.
6. The bear ______________ his head out of the cave.

Answer Keys

Page 7

Page 8
Order may vary.

Page 13

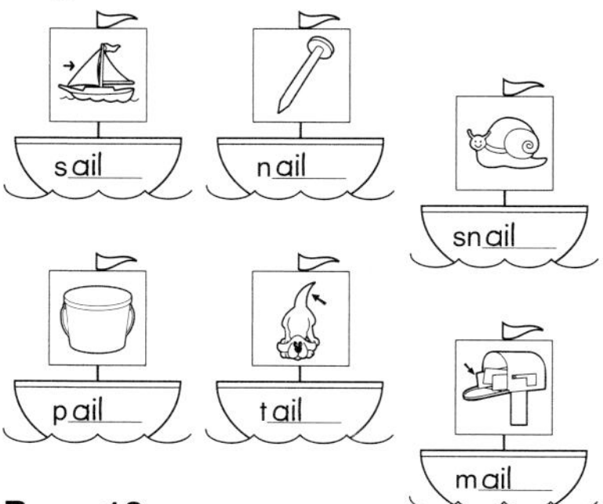

Page 18

1. snake
2. bake
3. rake
4. make
5. wake

Page 23

cap fap stap tap vap wrap
grap map flap dap plap trap
scap snap wap lap shap clap

Page 28

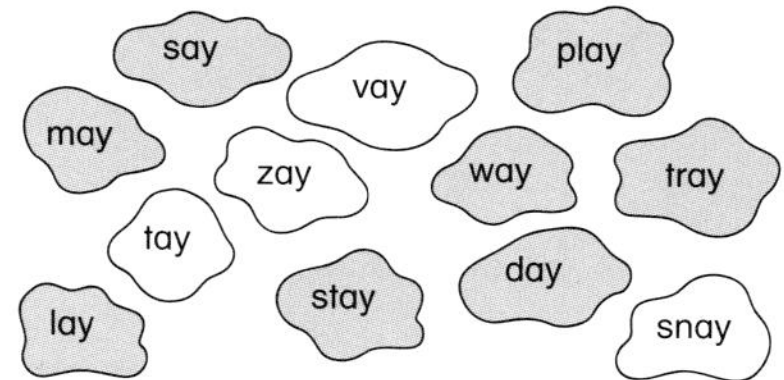

Order may vary.
1. may 2. say
3. play 4. tray
5. way 6. lay
7. stay 8. day

Page 32

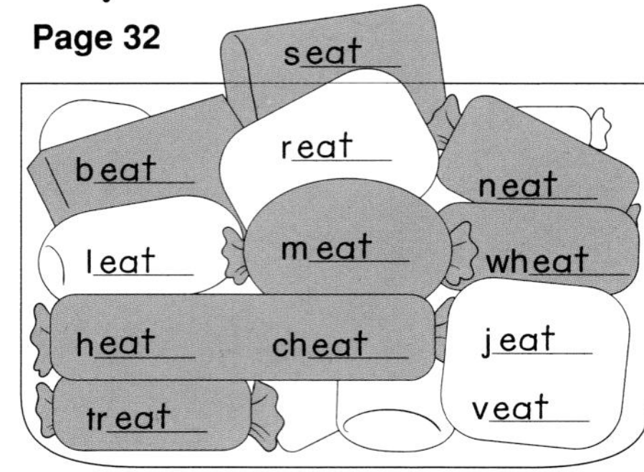

Order may vary.
1. seat 5. heat
2. beat 6. treat
3. neat 7. cheat
4. meat 8. wheat

Page 33

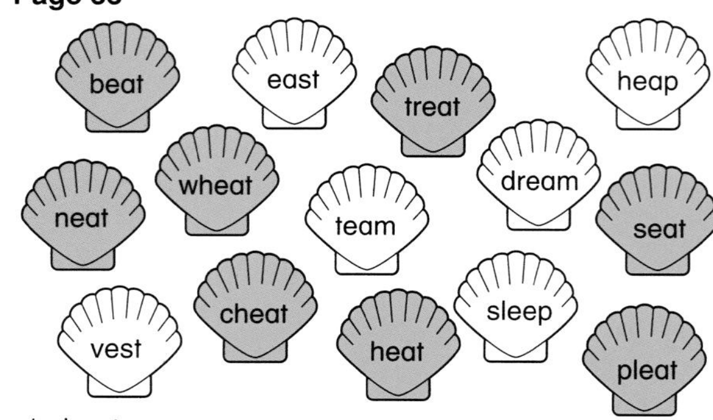

1. beat
2. cheat
3. neat
4. heat
5. treat

Page 38
Order may vary.

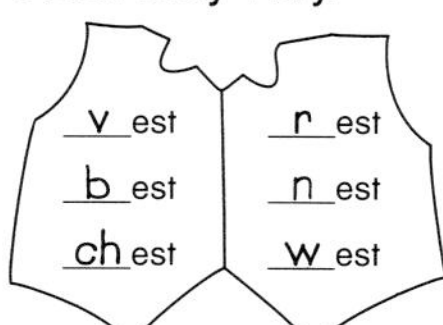

1. nest
2. chest
3. vest
4. rest
5. west
6. best

Page 43

chick sick pick
kick trick brick

1. pick
2. chick
3. brick
4. sick
5. kick
6. trick

Page 48

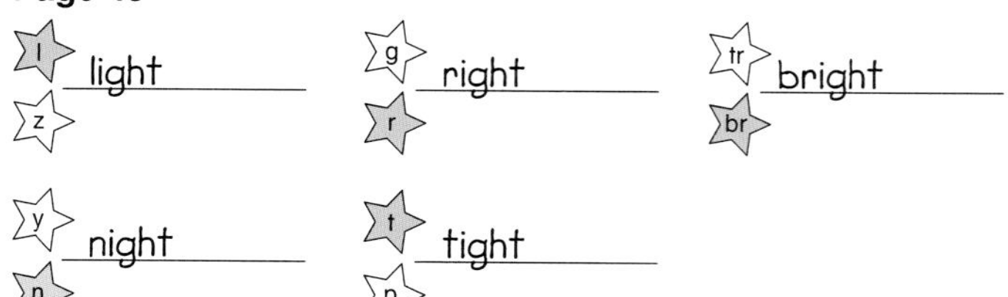

1. light
2. night
3. tight
4. bright
5. right

Page 52

	king	sing	ging
	qing	wing	jing
ving	hing	thing	fing
bring	sling	swing	pring
sting	fring	pling	cring
cling	string	ring	

Page 53

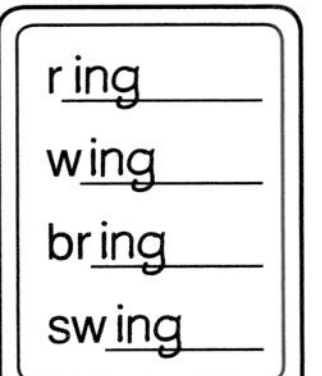

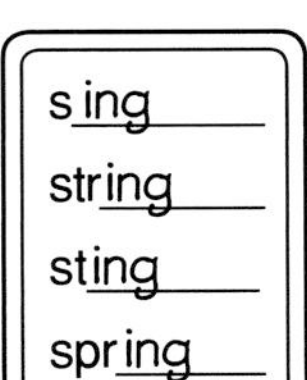

1. sing
2. sting
3. ring
4. bring
5. string
6. swing
7. wing
8. spring

Page 58

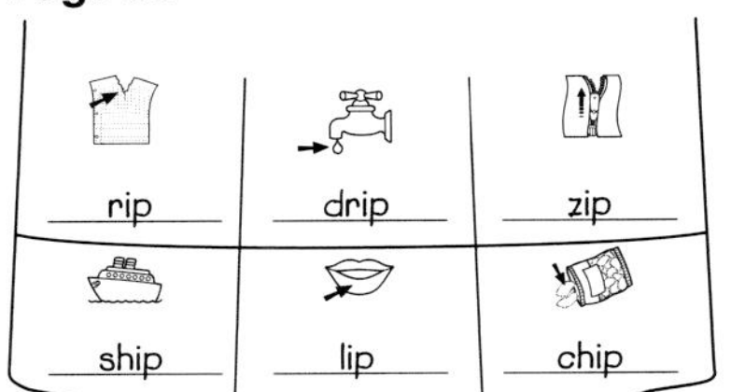

1. ship
2. chip
3. zip
4. rip

Page 63

Page 68

Order may vary.

pop	shop
top	stop
mop	hop
drop	plop

Page 73

best	lick	puck	duck	cluck		
say	ring	luck	flap	sick	bump	sip
		stuck	truck	buck	muck	hop
		cup	zip	nest	tuck	rock
		struck	yuck	pluck	suck	play

Page 77

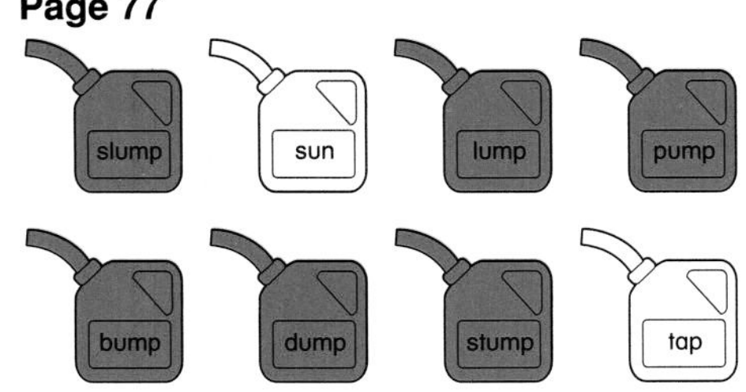

Order may vary.
1. slump
2. lump
3. pump
4. bump
5. dump
6. stump

Page 78

1. stump
2. hump
3. dump
4. jump
5. bump
6. pump

Page 79

-ack  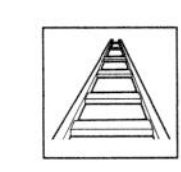 

tack track sack

-ick  

stick kick brick

Page 80

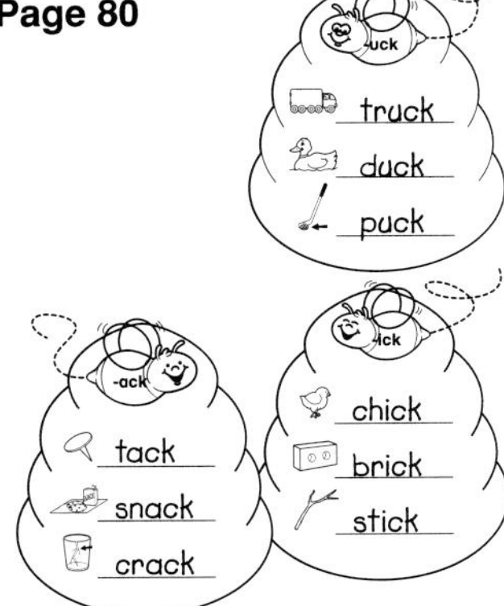

Page 81

1. clock
2. luck
3. back
4. knock
5. truck
6. chick
7. pick
8. quack

Page 82

1. rake
2. mail
3. sail
4. cake
5. shake
6. snail

Page 83

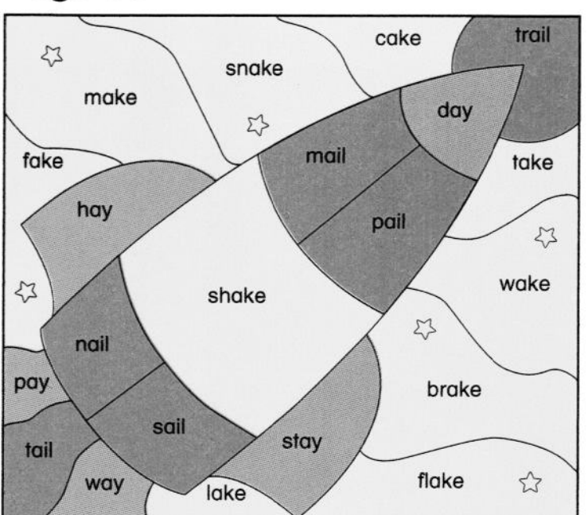

Page 84

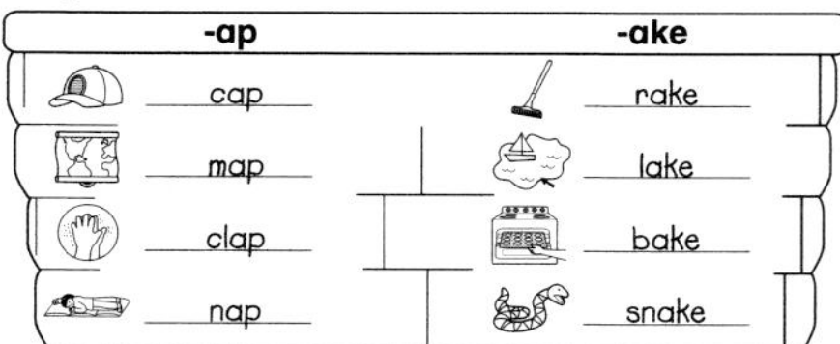

Page 85

1. map
2. stay
3. take
4. clap
5. day
6. lake
7. lap
8. bake

Page 86

Order may vary.

-ap	-ip
map	skip
clap	hip
trap	rip
lap	chip
snap	dip

Page 87

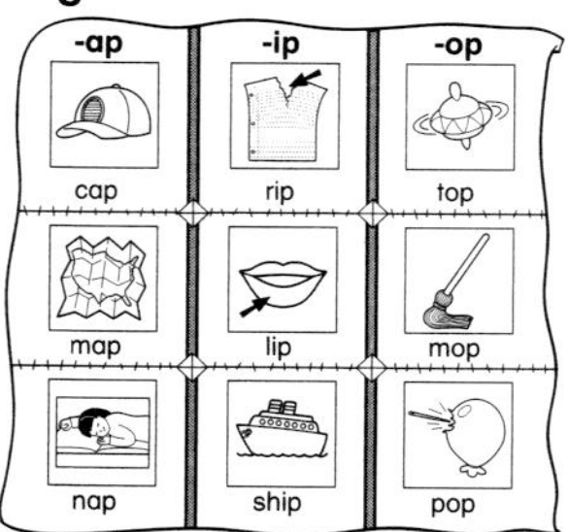

Page 88

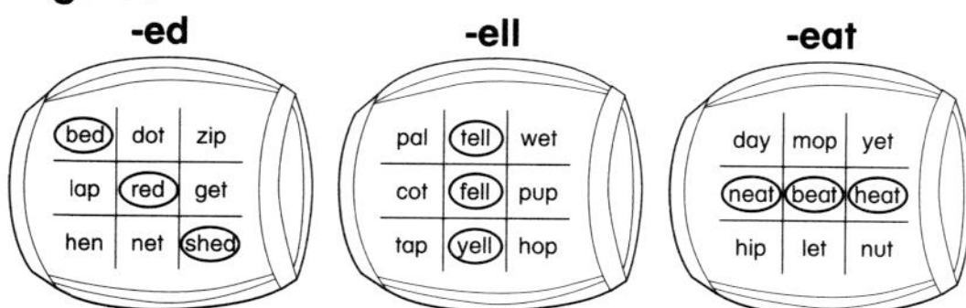

Order may vary.

-ed	-ell	-eat
bed	tell	neat
red	fell	beat
shed	yell	heat

Page 89

Order may vary.

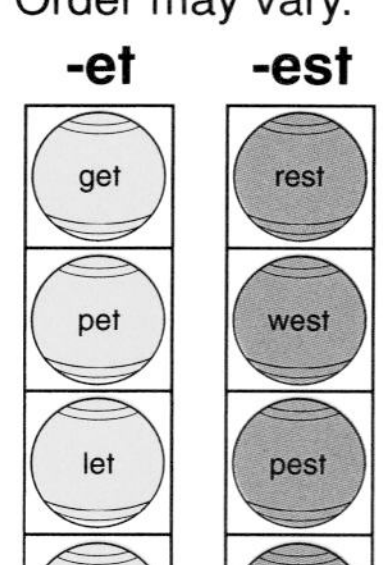

1. met
2. pet
3. best
4. pest
5. rest

Page 90

Order may vary.

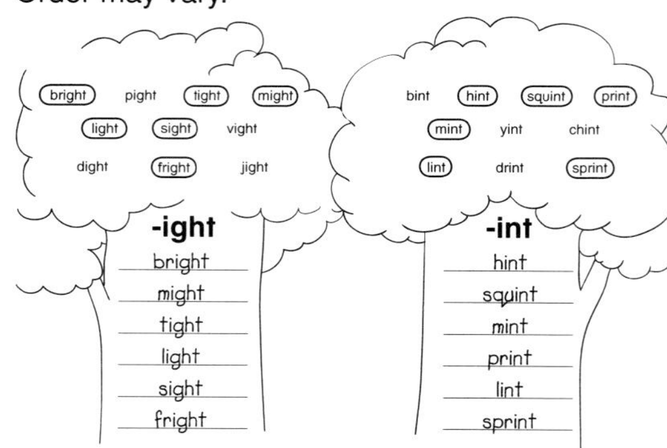

Page 91

-ip	-ick	-ing
drip	thick	wing
hip	pick	sing
flip	lick	bring

h	a	o	t	m	l	i	c	k
i	s	x	h	b	r	i	n	g
p	w	u	i	c	d	r	i	p
o	i	e	c	w	a	o	t	e
b	n	r	k	m	p	i	c	k
l	g	j	s	i	n	g	x	u
e	r	m	f	l	i	p	z	o

Page 92

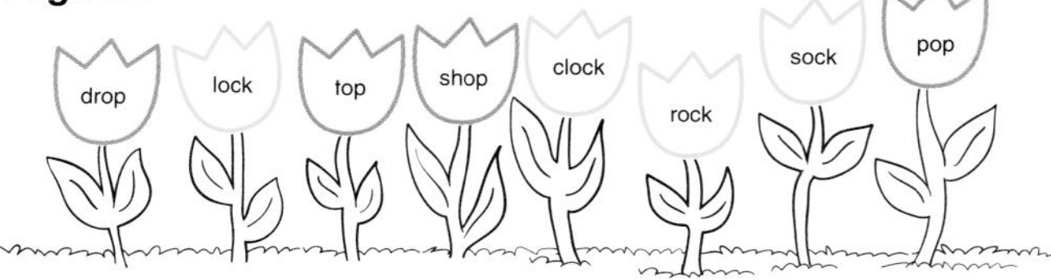

Order may vary.

-op	-ock
drop	lock
top	clock
shop	rock
pop	sock

Page 93

Order may vary.

-uck		
duck	tuck	stuck

-ump		
jump	pump	bump

1. duck
2. jump
3. bump
4. tuck
5. pump
6. stuck